BASS VIRTUOSOS

CONTENTS

Cover Art by Levin Pfeufer

Cherry Lane Music Company
Director of Publications/Project Editor: Mark Phillips
Publications Coordinator: Rebecca Skidmore

ISBN 978-1-60378-039-1

Visit our website at www.cherrylaneprint.com

An Interview with Jaco Pastorius (1987)

by Chuck Jacobs

You've been instrumental in changing the role of the electric bass, innovating new sounds, and bringing the bass more into the forefront of the music. How did you happen to come to create these changes?

It just happened naturally. First of all, I basically consider myself a rhythm and blues player and a jazz player. Rhythm and blues and jazz were the gigs that I would play when I was a kid, in nightclubs. For instance, you took my place on the C.C. Riders Band. [Wayne Cochran & the C.C. Riders. Around 1971 I had the ominous task of trying to fill Jaco's shoes in that band.] Then there were cocktail piano gigs, maybe a quartet with a saxophone, where I would play upright and Fender. So I was always playing more or less what I'm doing now. With regards to "being in the forefront," what got me playing like I do is that what I heard from people playing on bass, as far as a solo instrument, was not very much. I remember that one of the first jazz records I had when I was real young was this old Max Roach record. Just bass, two horns and Max [on drums]. I couldn't even tell what the bass was playing, because it was an old record and because the fidelity was bad. So I learned all the horn lines. All of a sudden I was fifteen and playing "Yardbird Suite" and "Confirmation" because that's what I figured out.

Were there any times when you played for others that your style wasn't accepted? Did you ever get hassled about it?

Oh, all the time…Still do. [laughs]

Did you ever lose gigs because of this?

I remember once I was working at Criteria [Studio in Miami] and somebody detrimentally said I was the John McLaughlin of the bass. That was kind of wild.

What gave you the impetus and desire to keep doing what you were doing?

Knowing that I was definitely on to something new. I worked very hard at it. Plus, I've worked with lots of people. I went out when I was very young. I seem to have a real natural talent for it. I also play drums, piano, guitar, flute, and sax.

Didn't you work with Ira Sullivan [sax and trumpet virtuoso] for a while?

Oh yeah, after I left Cochran's band, I worked with Ira, off and on for about two or three years. We were together every night for over a year.

Did you feel that period was at all formative in your playing?

Definitely. He's one of my biggest influences, one of my best friends, and I really dig him. I really enjoy his playing.

What do you feel the primary function of a bass player in a group should be?

Bottom. Like with the stuff I play, all this virtuoso type stuff, the whole time I'm totally conscious of the bottom. You'll never miss the bottom if you listen to what I'm doing.

Who has the ultimate responsibility for the timekeeping chores in a group, the bass or the drums?

I feel that the drums should have more. But I feel that lots of times bass players have to keep the time more because drummers have such rotten time sometimes. [laughs] The really good drummers have great time, but when they're coming up, drummers often rely on the bass player to lay the time down. I'm usually the timekeeper in any band I'm in.

There seem to be various viewpoints on who should have control of a group, regarding the volume, the intensity, etc. Who do you feel should ideally be the control factor in a group?

I feel that everybody in the group has an equal part, but I'll tell you right now that the bass player, any good bass player, should be the leader of any band. Not only rhythmically but harmonically you've got control over it, which drums can't have. Bass is a very unique and a very opportunistic place to be. You can have total harmonic control, and of course rhythmic control and time control, especially in jazz. The bass player has the time, because that lets the drummer play around you, which is what I've always liked. That's freedom for a drummer.

A lot of things have been said and written about your sound, and of course it is a unique sound. What do you feel makes it unique?
Well, I was probably the first guy to come on the scene with a fretless bass, which gives that singing sound. I've been doing it longer than other people, so maybe just maturity, and definitely my hands. It's in the hands; there are no special electric things. I just use a regular old Fender Jazz bass.

When you play in the studio, do you plug your bass directly into the board?
Usually. On my first album I mostly used my amp and a little direct. [Jaco uses an Acoustic 360 amp.] Since then, I usually go direct because it's easier. Plus, boards in studios have gotten a lot better, so that you

PHOTOGRAPHY BY ROBERT MINKIN

really don't even need amps and stuff. The outboard stuff has gotten much hipper.

How do you set up your controls on your bass?
I hardly ever use the front pickup. Once in a while I'll do it just to create a different sound, but usually what I do, when I want less bass, is turn down the treble on the back. In other words, my back pickup is up all the way all the time, and I just turn the tone control down.

What do you feel has made you a successful bassist?
Balls!! [laughs] You've got to learn a lot about music, you've got to learn lots of tunes; that's what you've got to do. I learned how to play by listening to records and the radio mostly. I didn't know how to read until I was in my early 20s. To learn every possible style of music I played everything. I played country and western for a year. I played shows off and on for five or six years. I would suggest that you learn how to read and really get into it.

What part do you feel attitude and/or personality play in the success of a bass player?
A lot. You've got to know how to talk to people, for one thing. A musician like me, doing what I'm doing, I'm not playing sessions or anything like that; I'm staying alive by just blowing. You've got to be very diplomatic and have a good sense of humor too.

How does a person develop a musical personality or style?
I feel technique plays a big role. There are certain things, facility wise, I do that I know nobody else can do. These are things I've worked on. Plus there's lots of things I do that I know other bass players can't do because their hands aren't as big. Attacking with your right hand also contributes to creating a sound or style.

You were one of the first people to exploit the full range of harmonics on the electric bass. What prompted you to do that, and how did you get into it?
When I first started playing, I was tuning the bass with the harmonics and they sounded good, so I just got into playing more of them. I figured out what all of them were musically and where they could be

produced. I figured out what every single note was. Then I started putting them into things—like you can run scales up and down the neck with harmonics, but you have to jump over every string to go diatonically.

How did you happen to get into playing the false or controlled harmonics?

Some guitar player showed me when I was very young. I was about 15 or so. He showed me how he did it by holding his finger lightly on the string and plucking the note with his thumb. Now I do it with my thumb and pluck with my finger. I used the exact same principle as an open string. Then I took my left hand and used it as if it were a capo, and then just measured it in half and plucked at that point. At that point I also produce all the natural harmonics on that note. It's very mathematical. I think very pragmatically and mathematically when I play. When I learn how to play tunes, for instance, I learn them in a particular key, like "Misty" is in E-flat. But if someone plays it in C, I can do it just as well because when I learn changes I just think of them as numbers. I and V for the corresponding scale positions. If you do this, you can easily transpose anything.

Do you feel that a player impugns his musical integrity or dignity by playing commercial music?

I don't think so. It really comes down to whether you play it well or not. If you do play it well, that's all you need to be concerned with.

In what ways, if any, do you change your playing from live to in the studio?

I don't play as recklessly in the studio because, needless to say, it's being recorded. Onstage I move around a lot and work for the audience in a visual way. Onstage I'm not as worried about every note I'm playing. In the studio you've really got to dig in.

How often do you like to change strings? [Jaco uses round wounds.]

I usually like to have brand-new strings. I like to change strings before every show. Sometimes when I'm doing two shows a night and my hands are starting to get a little tired, say after about two weeks into the tour, maybe I won't change strings as often then because my hands start to get a little torn up, especially my picking hand. But once I'm warmed up, I like to change them before every gig, because of the harmonics mostly. The harmonics start getting flat when the string gets old.

When you started out did you have any favorite bass players or early influences?

Bernard Odum [bass player on so many early James Brown hits], Gerald Jermott, Duck Dunn, James Jamerson of course, Pops Popwell, Ray Brown, Ron Carter, Gary Peacock. All these cats influenced me early on.

What instrument would you play if you couldn't play bass?

Drums probably, but that's not a fair answer because I also play drums. Maybe I'd like to play the bassoon because it's got the same timbre and range that I get on my Fender bass.

Is there anything that you'd like to tell young bass players starting out?

If you have the opportunity, you should work out on drums and piano. I think that's essential for every bass player, because you get the harmonic concept and you get the rhythmic concept. Also don't do any drugs or drinking or anything, at least until you're much older and know what you're doing, because it will not help you at all. When I was a young kid, lots of my friends were phenomenal musicians but never got anywhere because they started getting high. So that's a definite waste of time. Listen to as much music as you can, all different types. And learn how to read. Practice with cello books because they're really good for you as a bass guitarist. There really weren't any bass books to study, so I got legitimate cello books—Dotzauer's *113 Studies for Cello*. It's in four different books. Check that stuff out. I've done tremendous trombone studies as well, but cello is much hipper because the cello is tuned in fifths and you get these incredible skips that are really good for your hands.

What question have I not asked that you really want to answer?

[pauses] Who do you think is going to win the Super Bowl?

Who do you think is going to win the Super Bowl?

Dolphins!! [laughs]

AMAZING GRACE

Traditional
Arranged by Victor Wooten

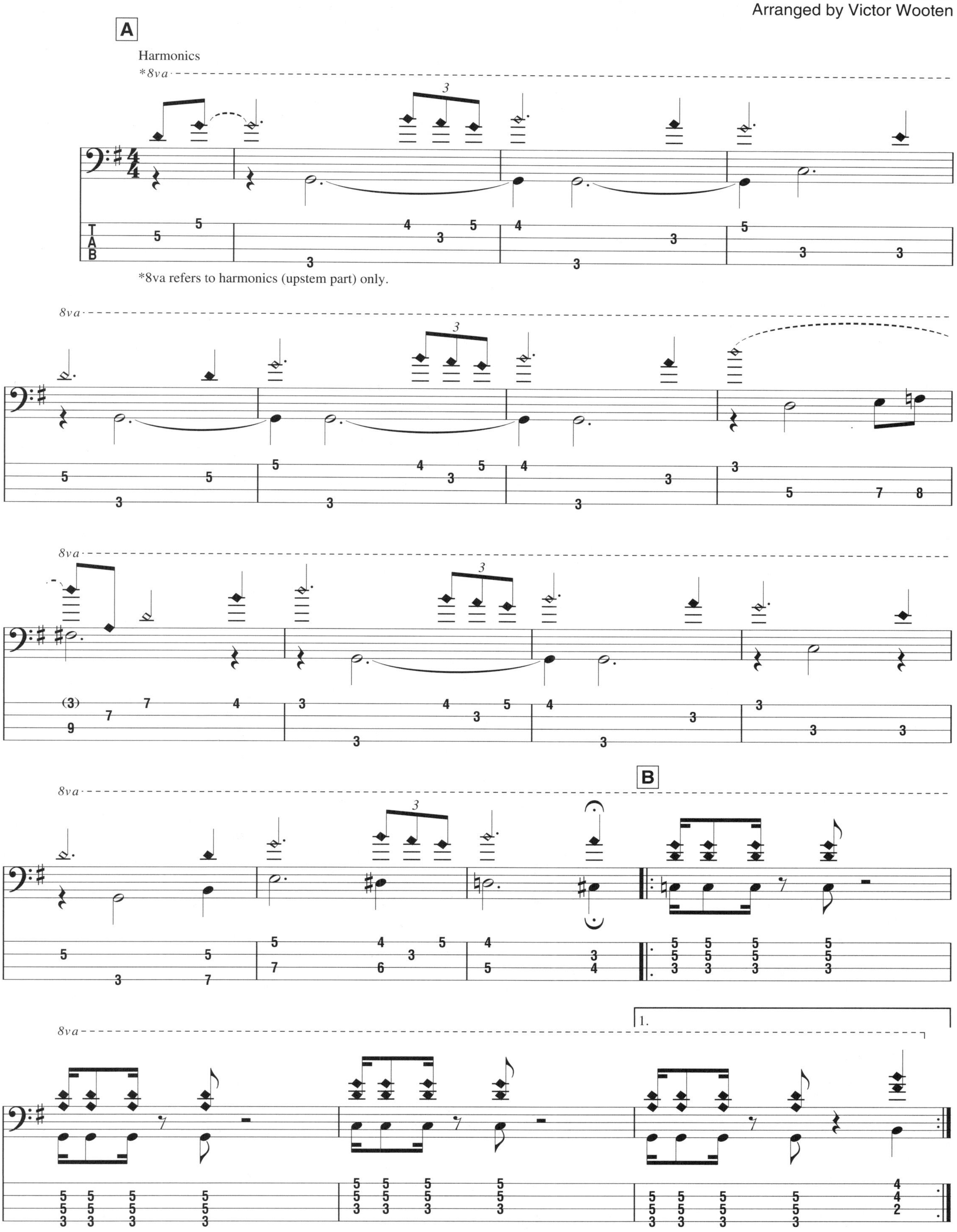

A
Harmonics
*8va
T
A
B
*8va refers to harmonics (upstem part) only.
8va
B
1.

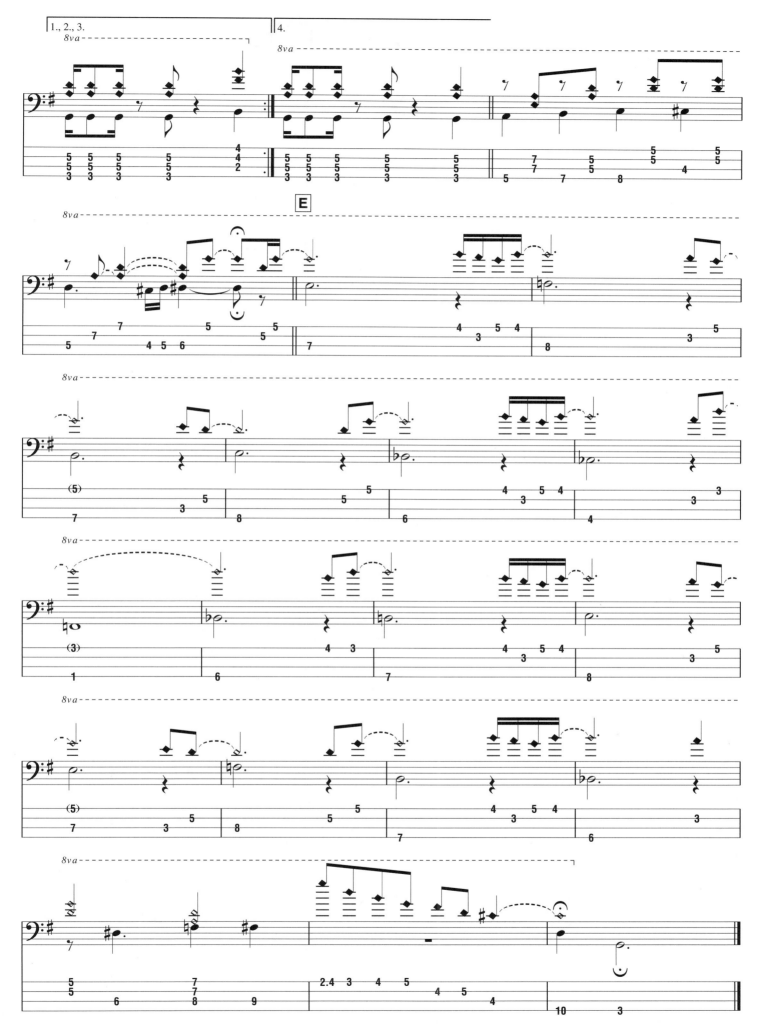

BERNADETTE

Words and Music by
Brian Holland, Lamont Dozier
and Edward Holland

Tune down 1/2 step:
(low to high) Eb-Ab-Db-Gb

Intro
Moderately ♩ = 108

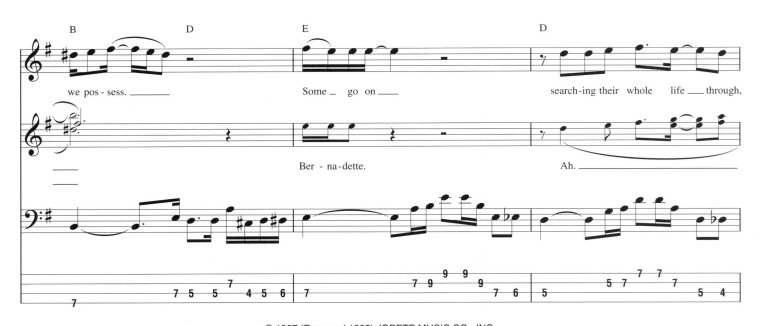

and — nev-er find — the love — I've found — in you. _____

End Voc. Fig. 1

(Ah.) _____ Ah.

Verse

1. And when I speak of you, I see en-vy in oth-er men's __ eyes.

Voc. Fig. 2

(I _____ want you to know.

And I'm well a-ware __ of what's on their minds. __

I _____ want you to know.

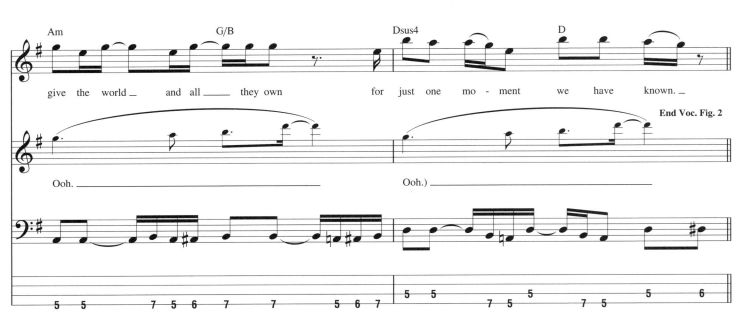

Chorus

Bkgd. Voc.: w/ Voc. Fig. 1

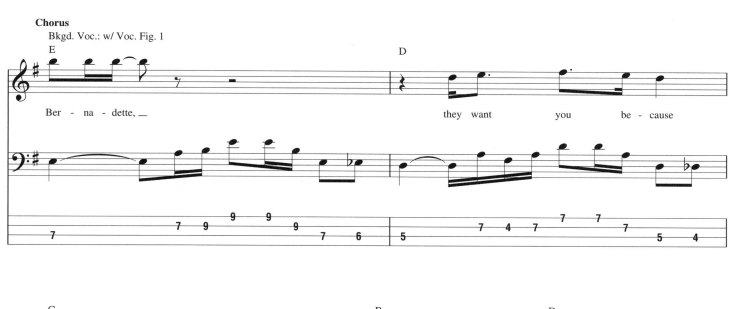

Ber - na - dette, __ they want you be - cause

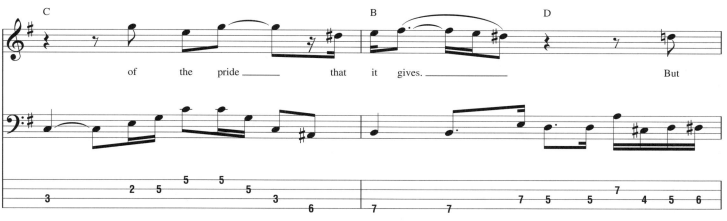

of the pride _____ that it gives. _____ But

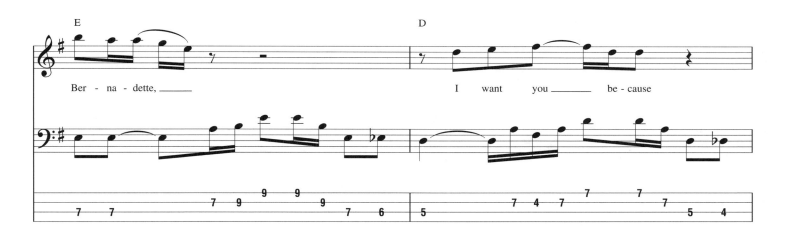

Ber - na - dette, _____ I want you _____ be - cause

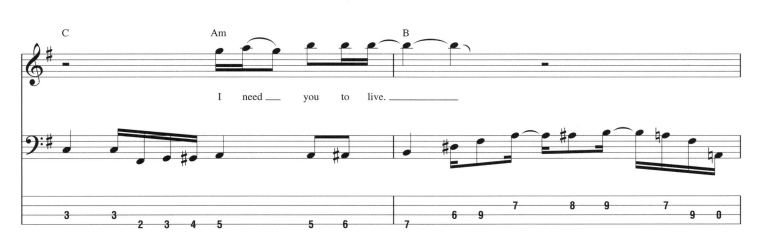

I need __ you to live. _____

13

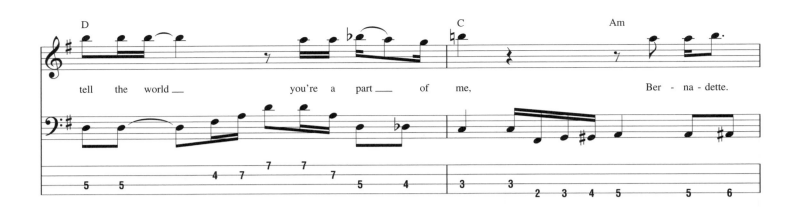

tell the world ___ you're a part ___ of me, Ber - na - dette.

Bridge

In your arms I find ___ the ___ kind of peace of mind ___ the world ___ is ___ search - ing ___

(In _____ your arms I find the kind of peace of mind the world is search - ing

___ for. ___ But you, you give __ me the joy this heart of mine has

for. You _____ give me the joy this heart of mine has

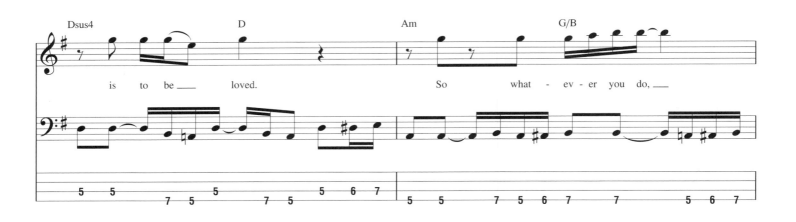

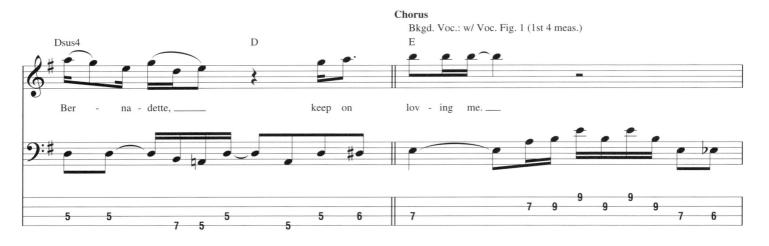

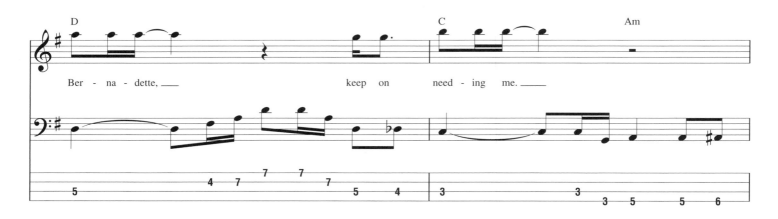

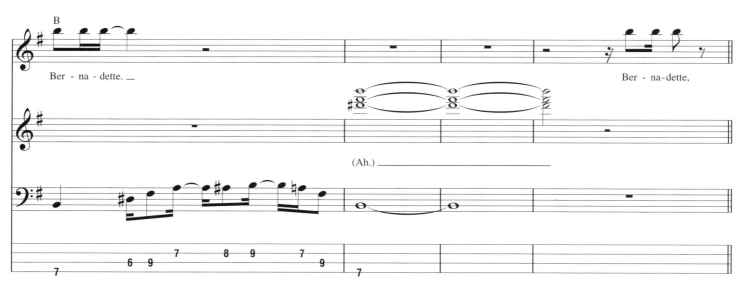

you're the   soul   of   me, ____   more than a ____

____ dream. ____ ____   You're ____ a   prayer ____   to   me. ____   And

Ber - na - dette, ____   you ___ mean   more   to   me ____   than a

wom-an ___   was   ev - er ____   meant ___   to   be. ____   Ber - na - dette, ____   my   dar - lin'. ____

17

BIRDLAND

Music by Josef Zawinul

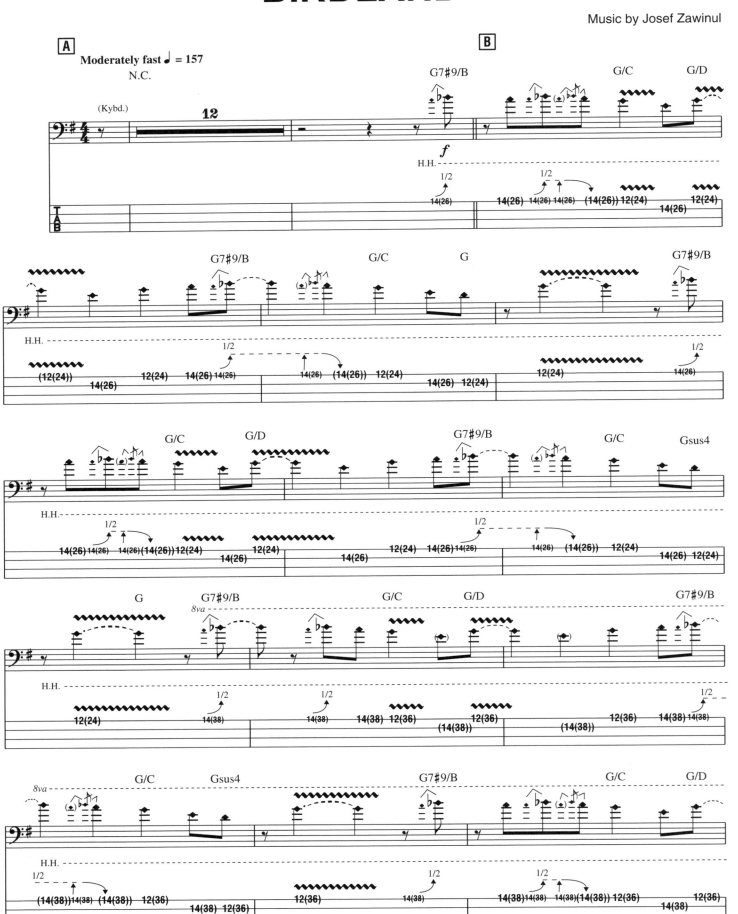

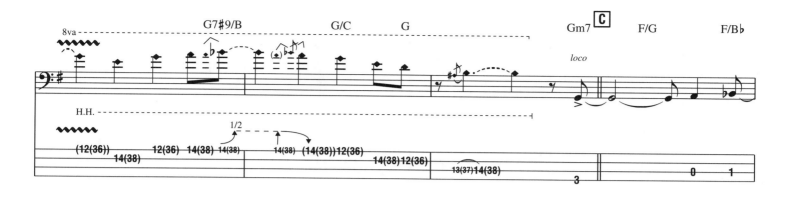

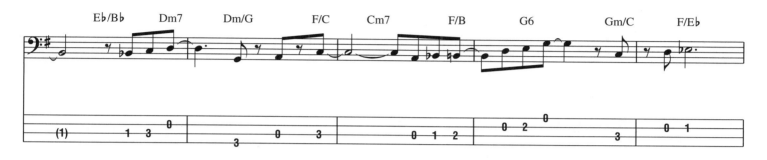

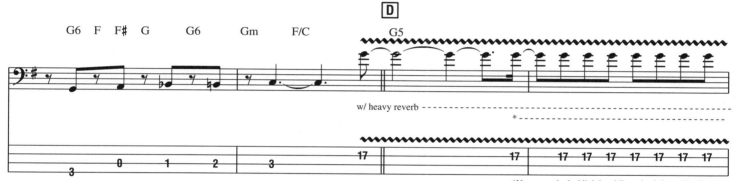

*Notes are plucked lightly while maintaining wide vibrato.

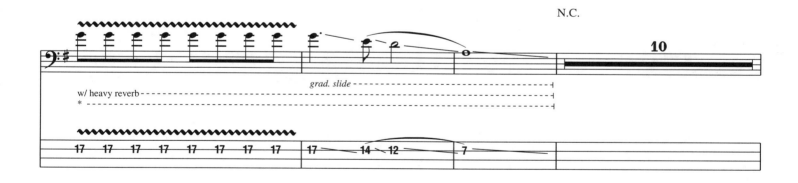

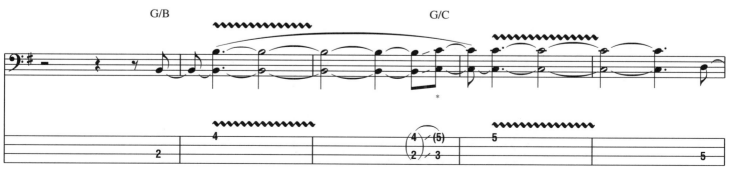

*The bottom note is plucked.

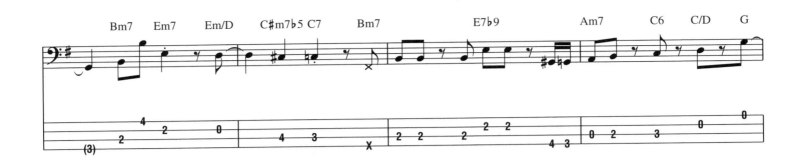

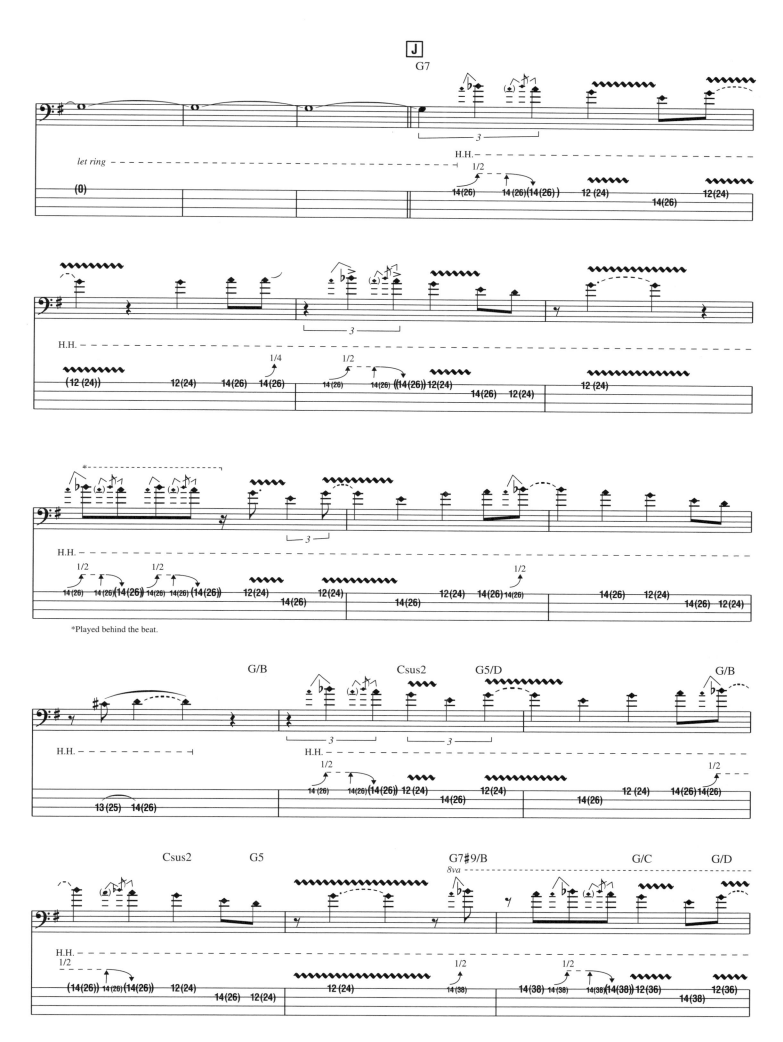

*Played behind the beat.

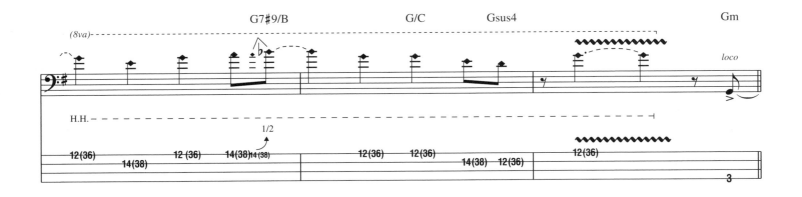

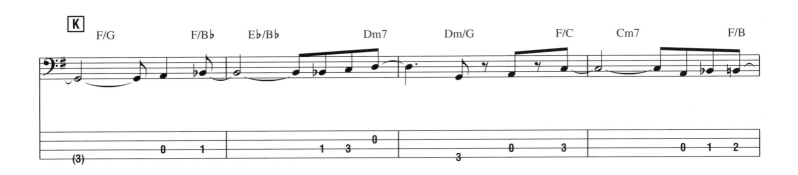

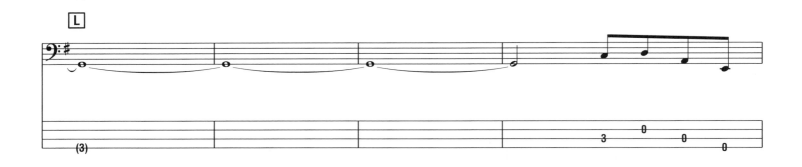

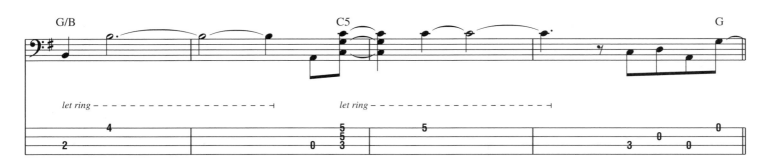

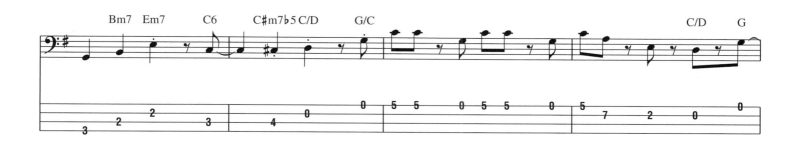

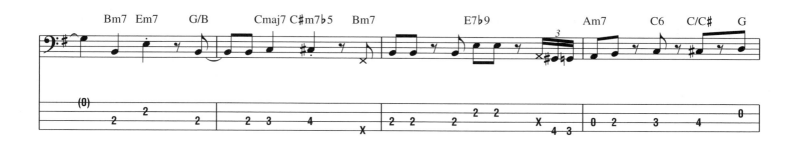

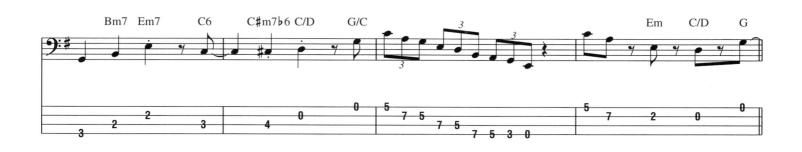

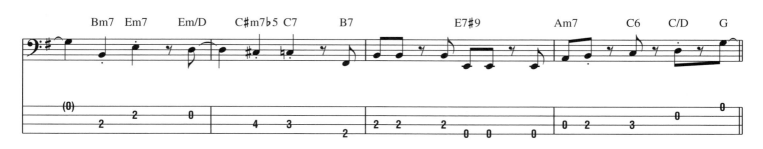

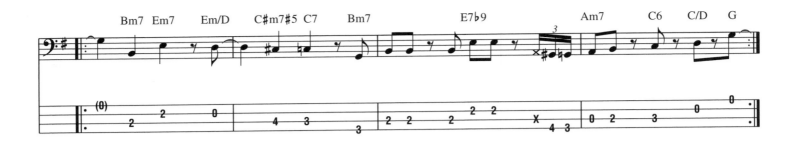

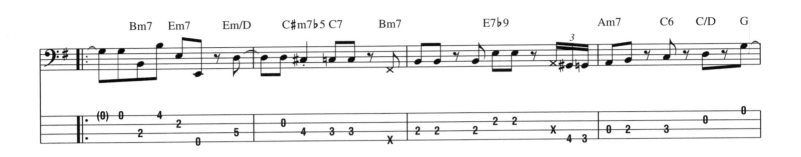

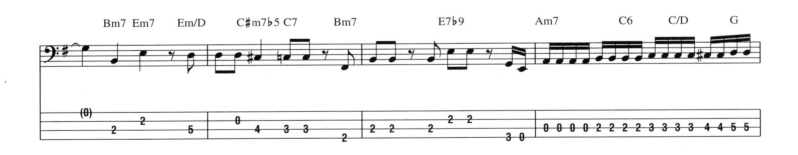

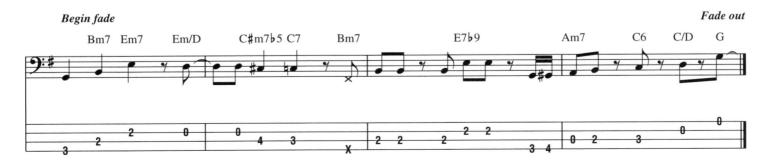

COYOTE

Words and Music by
Joni Mitchell

Intro
Fast ♩ = 164

*Cmaj9 C6sus4 Cmaj9 C6sus4

*Chord symbols reflect overall harmony. **8va refers to harmonics only (throughout).

Cmaj9 C6sus4 Cmaj9 C6sus4

Verse
Eb

1. (Spoken:) No regrets, Coyote.

Fmaj7/G Cmaj9

We just come _ from such dif-f'rent sets of cir-cum-stance. _ I'm up all night in stu-

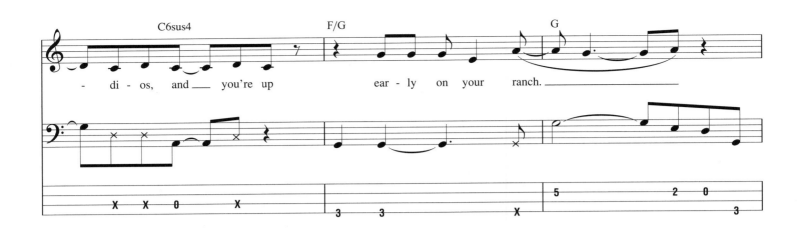

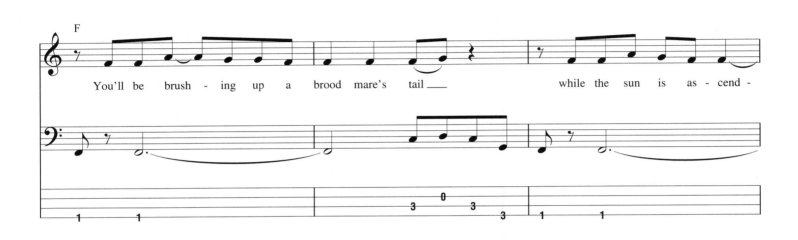

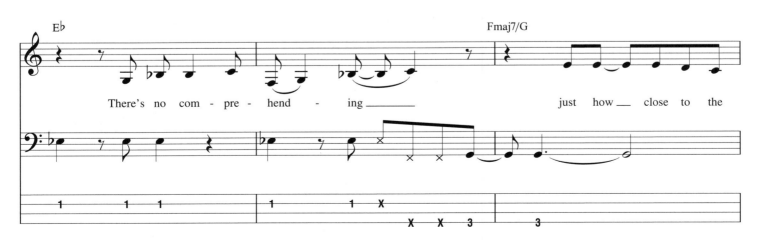

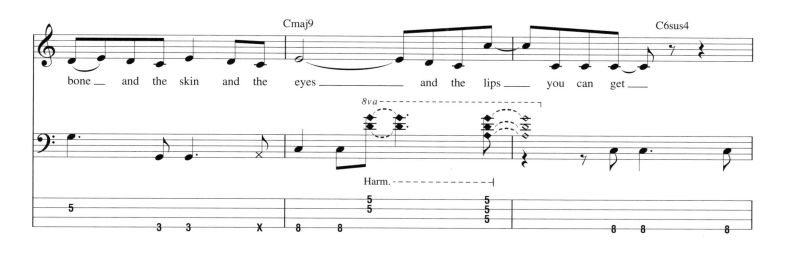

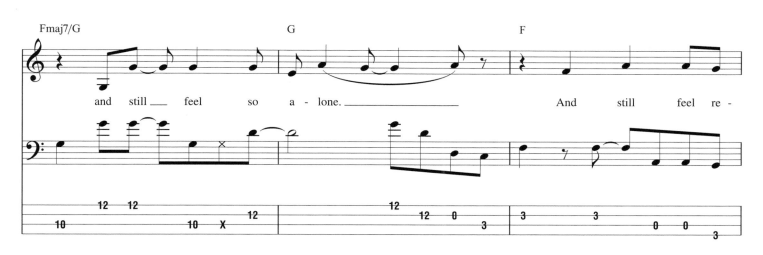

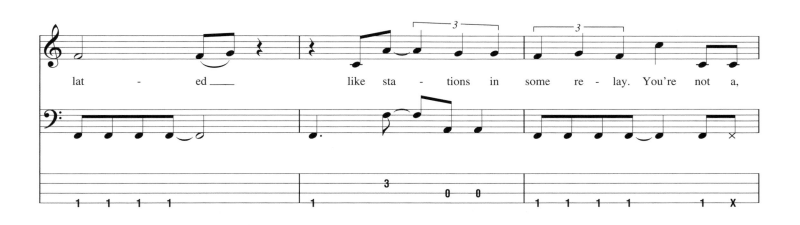

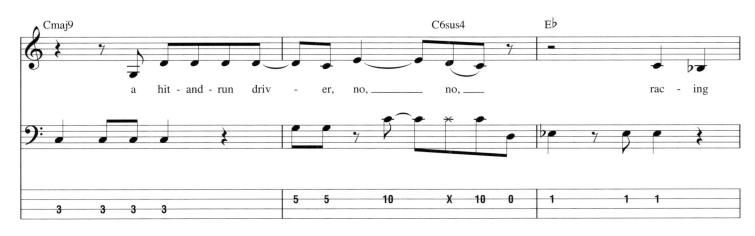

a - way.   You just picked up a hitch - er,

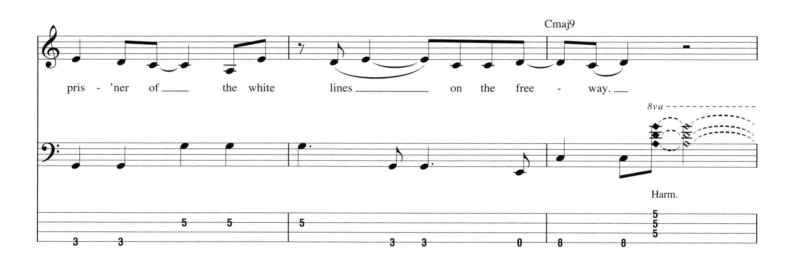

pris - 'ner of ___ the white   lines ___ on the free - way. ___

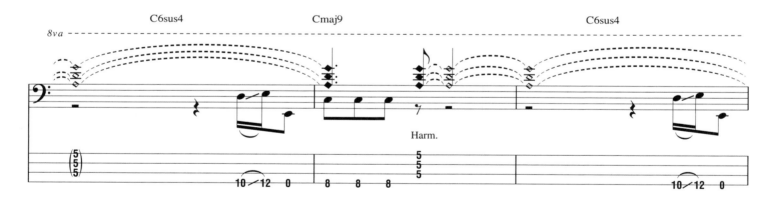

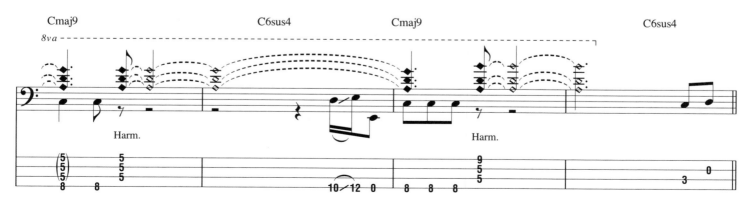

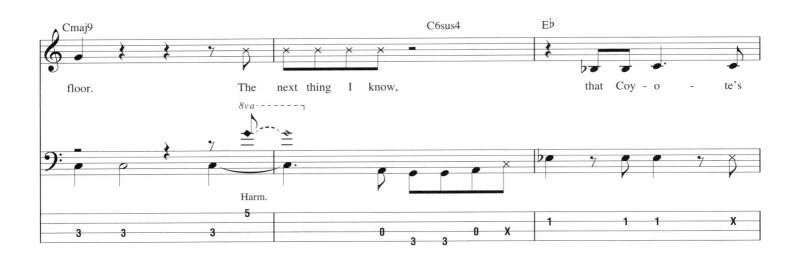

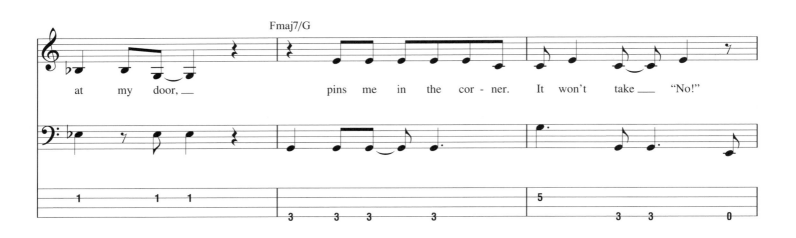

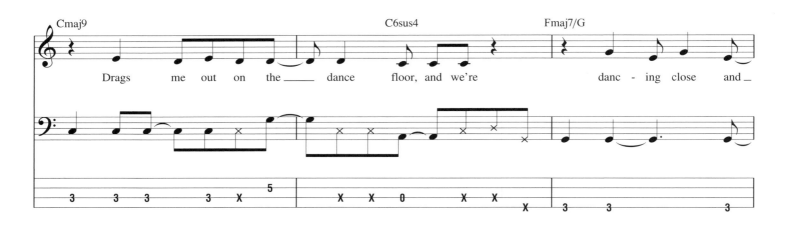

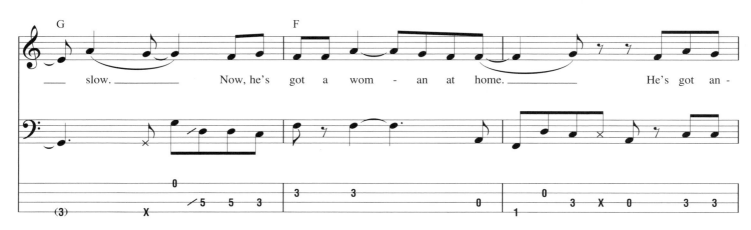

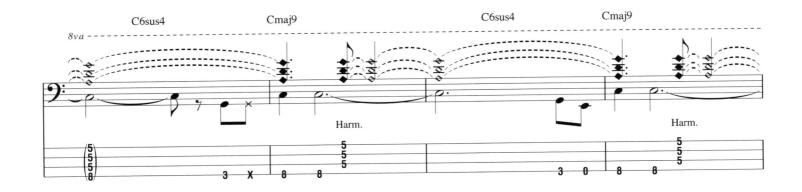

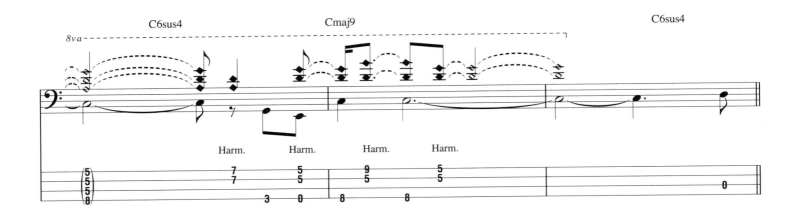

You just picked up a hitch - er, pris - 'ner of ___ the white lines ___ on the

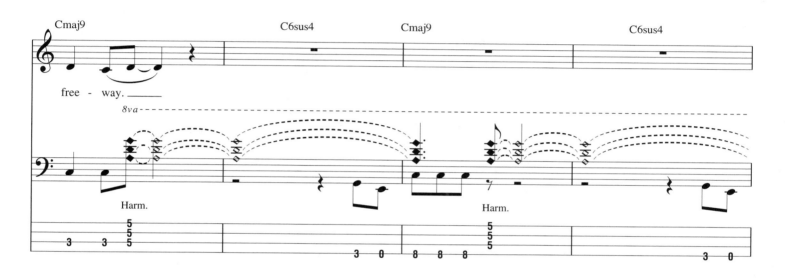

free - way. ___

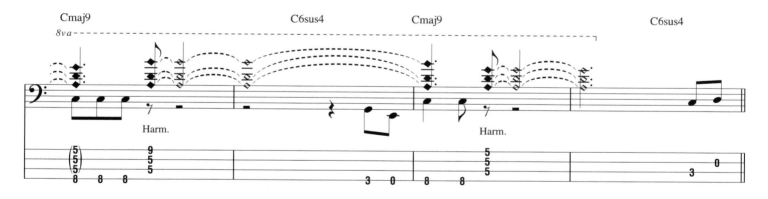

Verse

4. Coy - o - te's in the cof - fee shop. He's star - ing a hole in his

scram - bled eggs. ___   He picks up my scent on his fin - gers while he's

watch - ing the wait - ress - 's legs. ___   He's   too   far ___ from the Bay

of Fun - dy, ___   from Ap - pa - loo - sas and ea - gles ___ and tides. ___

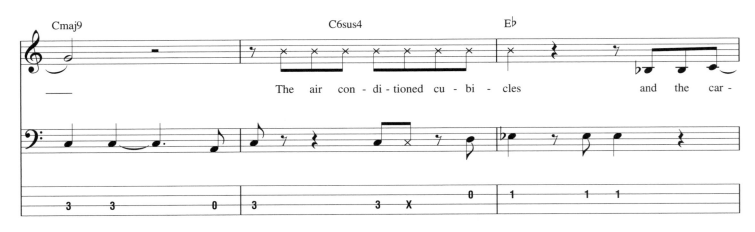

The air con - di - tioned cu - bi - cles   and the car -

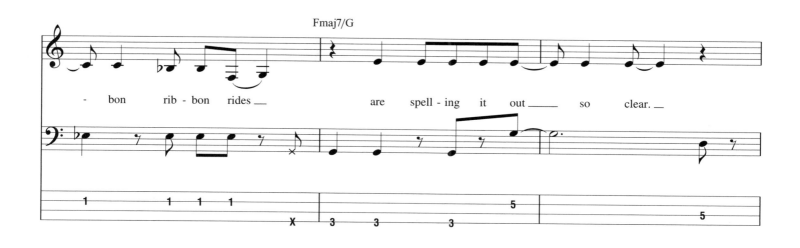

- bon rib - bon rides ___ are spell-ing it out ___ so clear. ___

Ei - ther he's gon - na have to stand ___ and fight ___ or take off ___ out of ___

___ here. _____ I tried to run a - way my - self, ___

to run a - way and wres - tle with my ___ e - go _____ and with this, ___

39

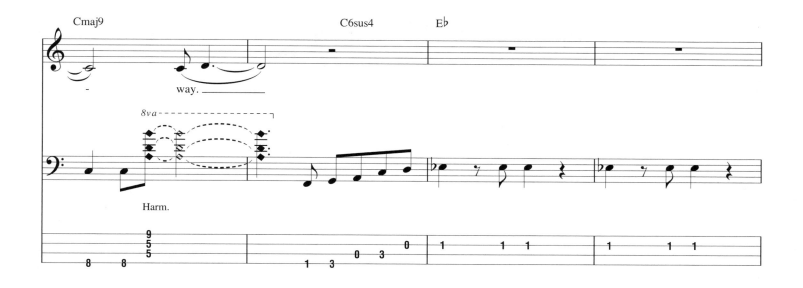

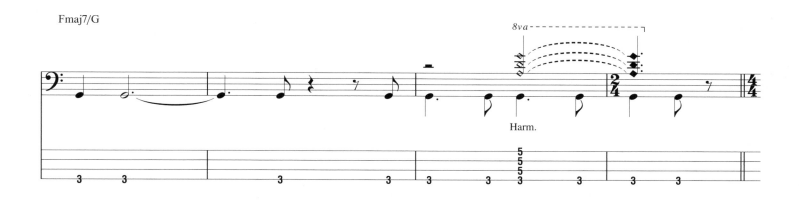

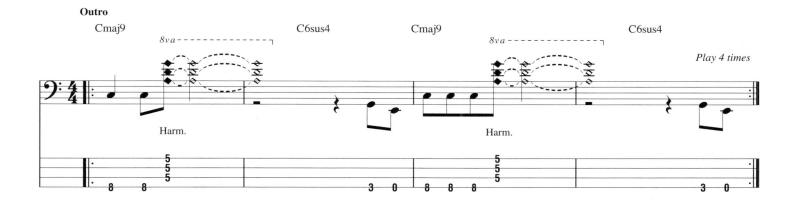

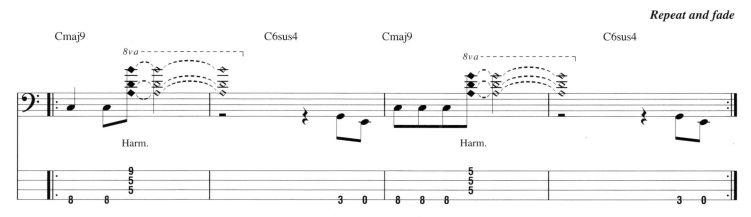

DIAMONDS ON THE SOLES OF HER SHOES

Words and Music by
Paul Simon
Beginning by Paul Simon
and Joseph Shabalala

as if ev-'ry-bod-y knows _____ what I'm talk-

w/ Bass Fig. 1 (3 times)

- ing a - bout, _____ as if ev - 'ry-bod-y here would know ex -

act - ly what I was talk - ing a - bout. I'm talk - in' 'bout

dia - monds on _____ the soles _____ of her shoes. _____

dia

- monds.

Interlude

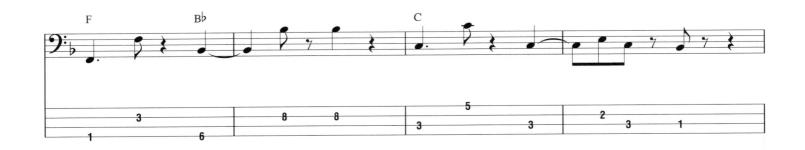

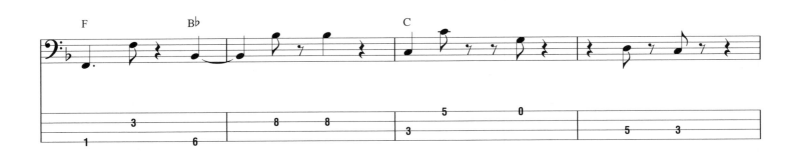

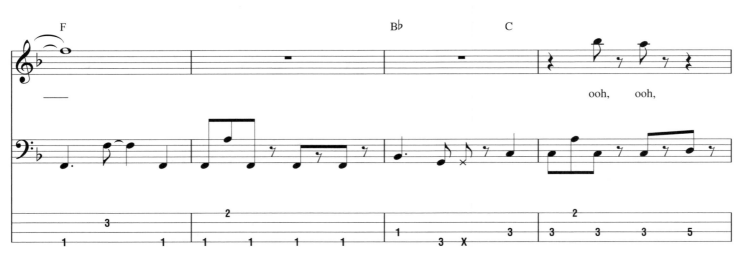

DMV

Lyrics by Les Claypool
Music by Les Claypool,
Larry LaLonde and Tim Alexander

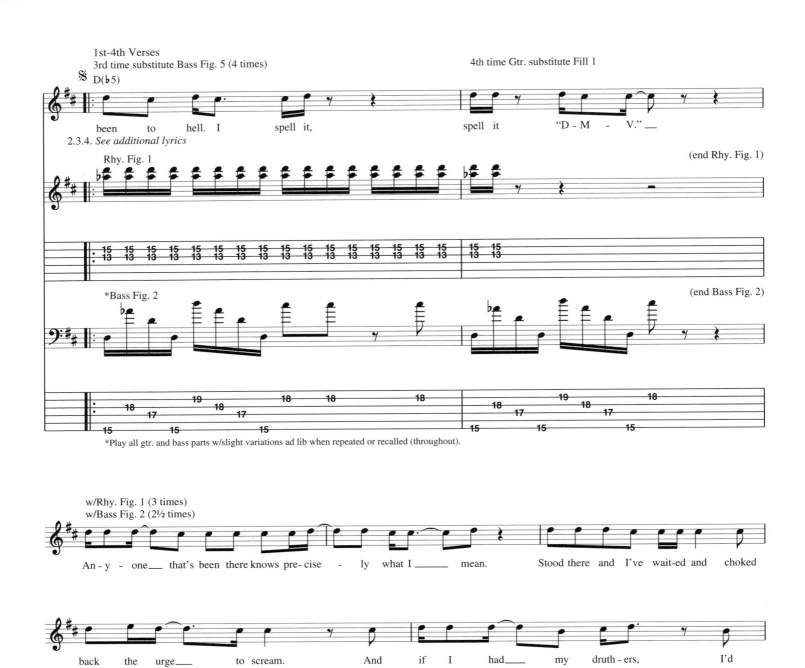

1st-4th Verses
3rd time substitute Bass Fig. 5 (4 times)

4th time Gtr. substitute Fill 1

been   to   hell. I   spell it,   spell it   "D - M - V." ___

2.3.4. *See additional lyrics*

Rhy. Fig. 1

(end Rhy. Fig. 1)

*Bass Fig. 2

(end Bass Fig. 2)

*Play all gtr. and bass parts w/slight variations ad lib when repeated or recalled (throughout).

w/Rhy. Fig. 1 (3 times)
w/Bass Fig. 2 (2½ times)

An - y - one___ that's been there knows pre- cise - ly what I _____ mean.   Stood there and I've wait-ed and   choked

back   the   urge___   to scream.   And   if   I   had___   my   druth - ers,   I'd

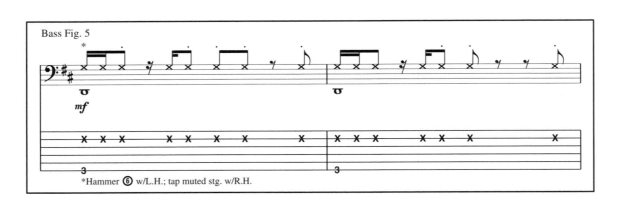

Bass Fig. 5

mf

*Hammer ⑥ w/L.H.; tap muted stg. w/R.H.

Fill 1

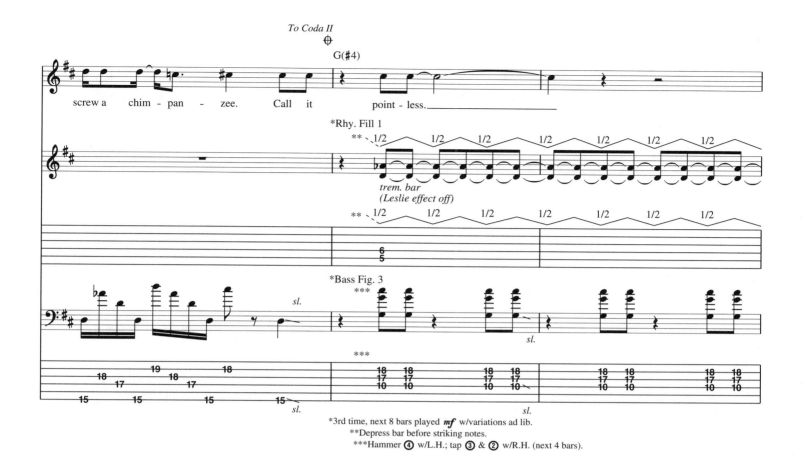

screw a chim-pan-zee. Call it point - less._____

*3rd time, next 8 bars played **mf** w/variations ad lib.
**Depress bar before striking notes.
***Hammer ④ w/L.H.; tap ③ & ② w/R.H. (next 4 bars).

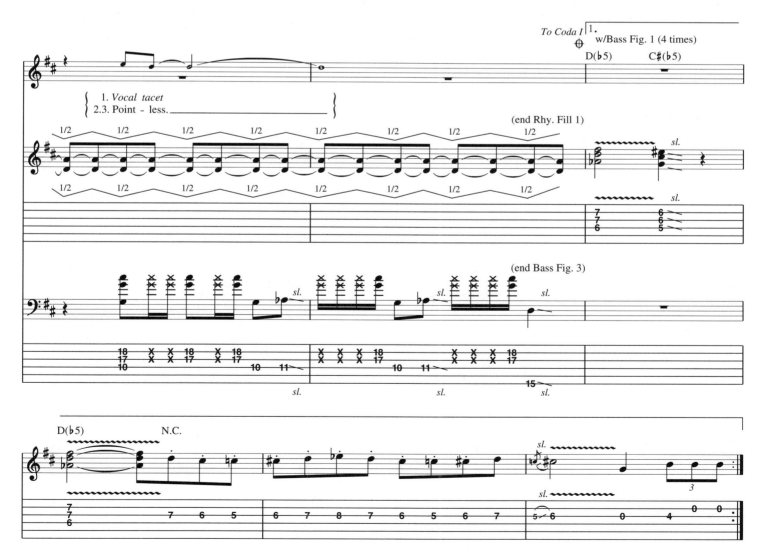

1. Vocal tacet
2.3. Point - less._____

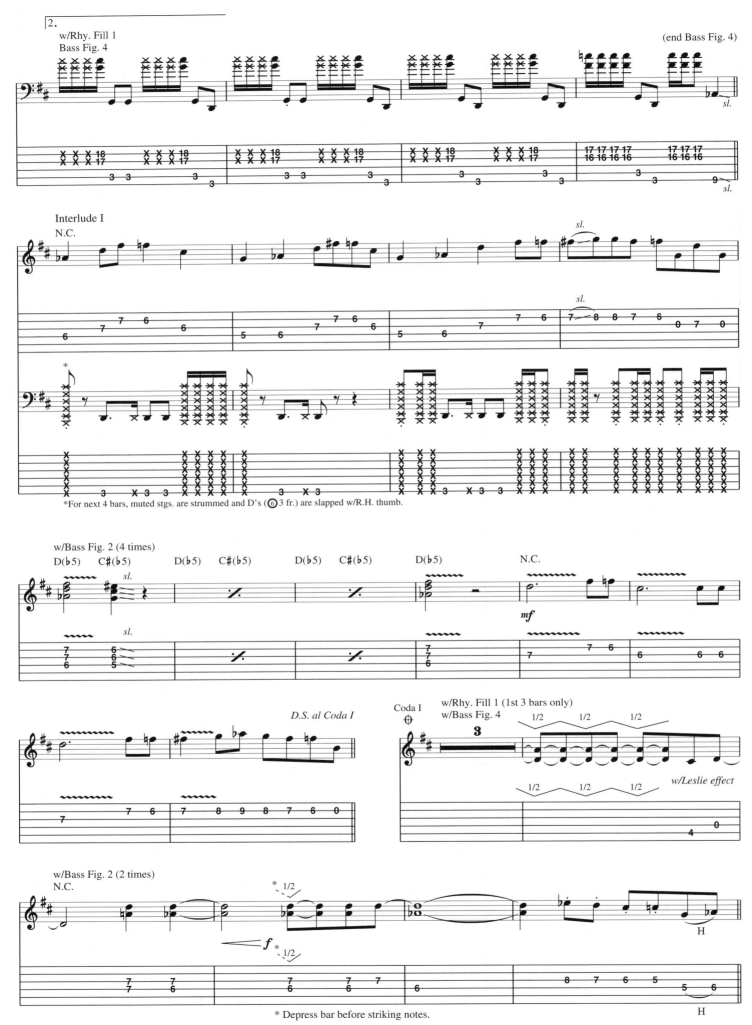

*For next 4 bars, muted stgs. are strummed and D's (⑥ 3 fr.) are slapped w/R.H. thumb.

* Depress bar before striking notes.

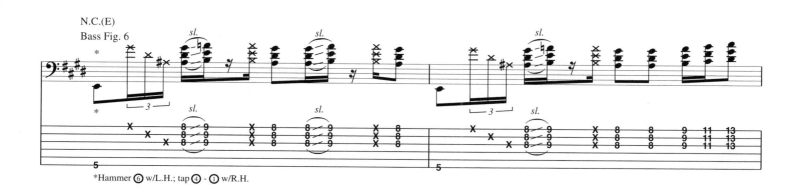

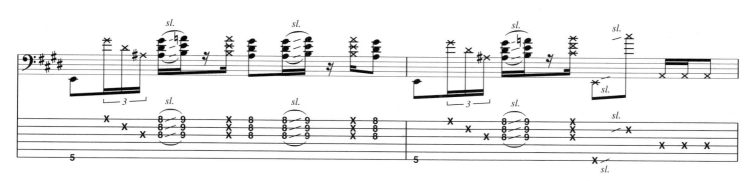

Outro solo
w/Bass Fig. 6
N.C.(E)

w/Bass Fig. 7
(A/E)

Bass Fig. 7

1.

2.

*Hammer ③ w/L.H.; tap ② & ① w/R.H.

54

Additional Lyrics

2. When I need relief, I spell it "THC."
   Perhaps you may know vaguely what I mean.
   I sit back and smoke away huge chunks of memory.
   As I slowly inflict upon myself a full labotomy.
   Call it pointless, pointless. *(To Interlude I)*

3. Barbecues, tea kettles, gobs of axle grease.
   There comes a time for every man to sail the seas of cheese.
   Now life's a bowl of bagel dogs, but there are unpleasantries:
   Cold toilet seats, dentist chairs and trips to DMV.
   Call it pointless, pointless. *(To Interlude II)*

4. I've been to hell. I spell it, I spell it "DMV."
   Anyone that's been there knows precisely what I mean.
   I've stood in line and waited near an hour and fifteen.
   And if I had my druthers, I'd screw that chimpanzee.
   Call it pointless, *etc.*

DONNA LEE

By Charlie Parker

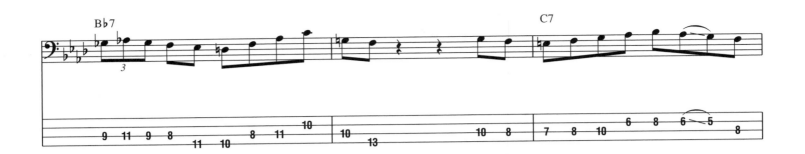

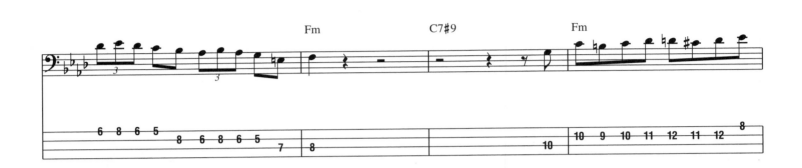

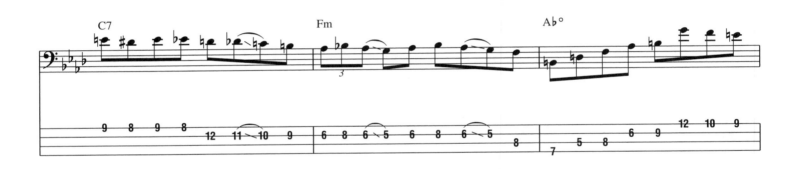

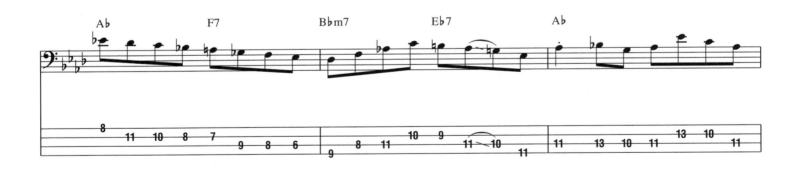

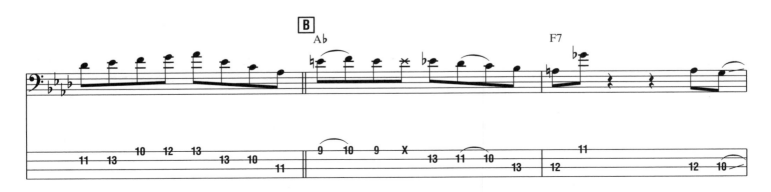

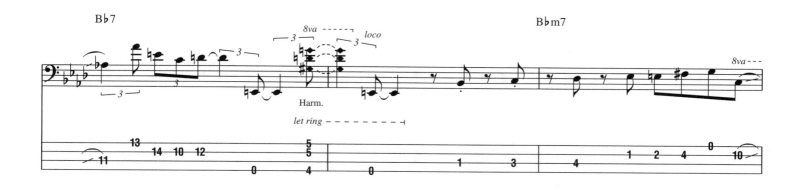

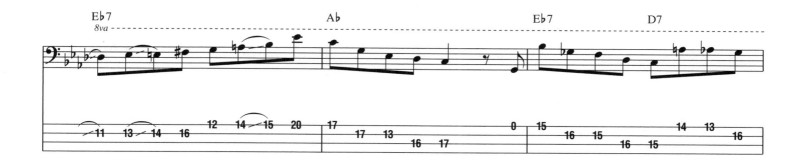

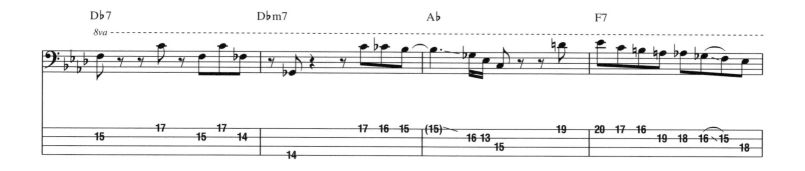

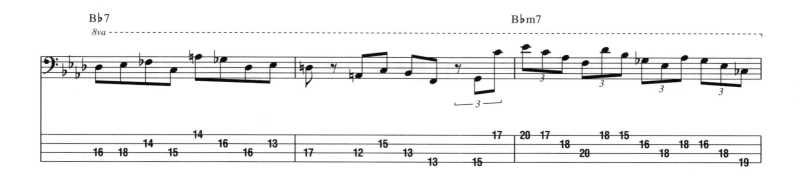

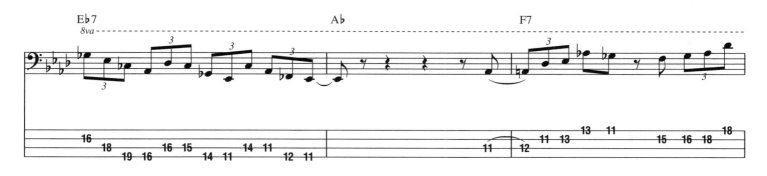

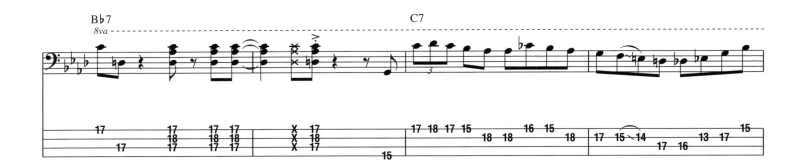

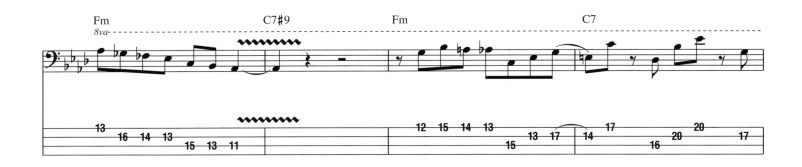

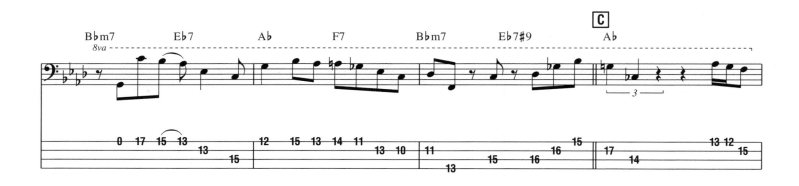

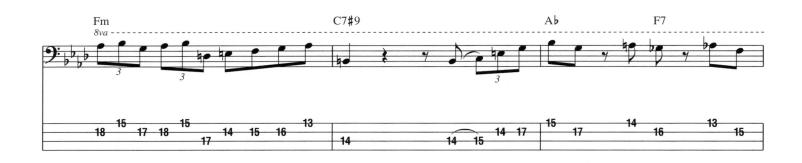

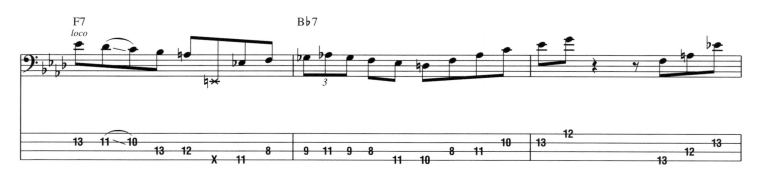

DOWN TO THE NIGHTCLUB

Words and Music by
Stephen Kupka, Emilio Castillo
and David Garibaldi

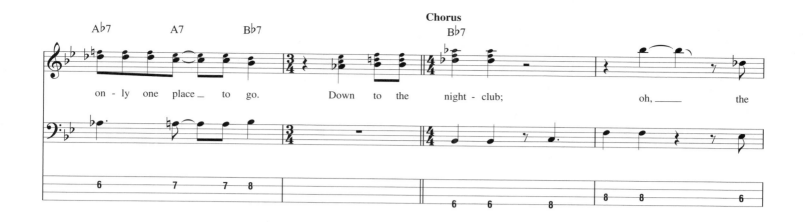

on-ly one place __ to go. Down to the night-club; oh, ____ the

wom-en be righ-teous-ly read-y and pret-ty. To the night-club, oh yeah, __

To Coda ⊕ |1. |2.

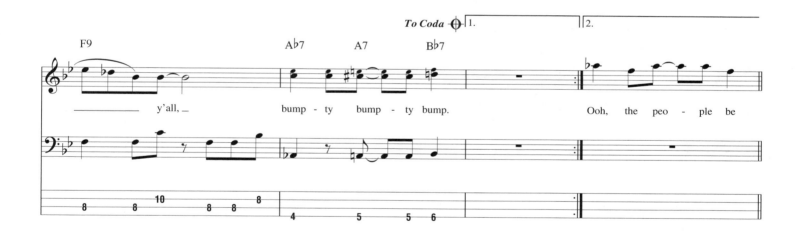

____ y'all, __ bump-ty bump-ty bump. Ooh, the peo-ple be

Bridge

bump-ing ____ (at Bump Cit-y). The joint be

jump - ing _____   (at Bump Cit - y).

Oh, the ma - ma's be _____ hump - ing _____   (at Bump Cit - y).

F9

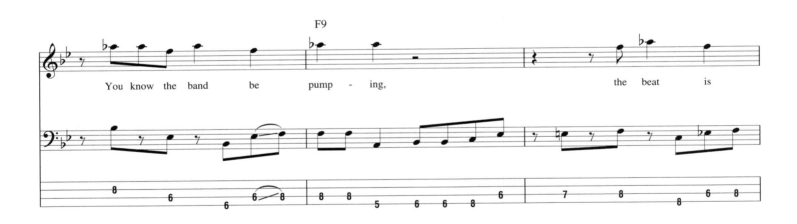

You know the band be pump - ing,   the beat is

some - thing.   Ooh, the band is pump - ing.   Woh! _____

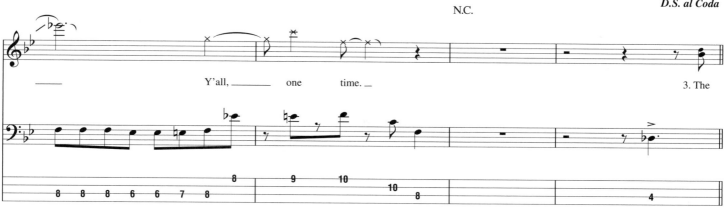

N.C.

Y'all, _____ one time. __

3. The

⊕ Coda

Outro

Bb7   Gbmaj7   Ab7   A7   Bb7

Down   to   the   night - club;   we   go   bump - ty   bump - ty bump.

Gbmaj7   Ab7   A7   Bb7

Down   to   the   night - club;   { we   be   slick,   slick, __   slick. }
                                      { tie   on   a   drunk,   drunk, __   drunk. }

w/ Lead Voc. ad lib

Bb7   Gbmaj7   Ab7   A7   Bb7

Down   to   the   night - club.

To the

67

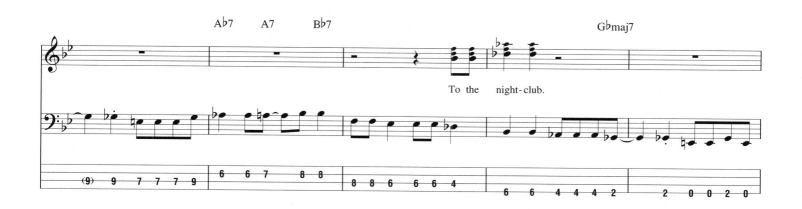

Additional Lyrics

2. Sitting by the dance floor, checking it out,
   Watching the man with the fast feet.
   He's got the hippest threads and the bad bugaloo,
   And a big old bag of tricks.

   2nd Chorus:
   Down to the nightclub.
   You can get what you want if you know where to find it.
   To the nightclub,
   We be slick, slick, slick. *(To Bridge)*

3. The night's almost gone and we're still going strong;
   The party's been so hearty.
   I hope it doesn't show while I'm driving down the road
   That I had too much to drink.

   3rd Chorus:
   Down to the nightclub.
   If you got the dough the liquor will flow.
   To the nightclub,
   Tied on a drunk, drunk, drunk. *(To Coda)*

FUNK ME TENDER

Music by Randy Coven

*T = R.H. tap

Ⓣ = L.H. tap

**Set dalay at 160 msec. w/single repeat.

Guitar solo

D.S. al Coda II

*Artificial harmonics created
by resting R.H. thumb on
string and plucking w/fingernail
(near bridge pickup).

GOODBYE PORK PIE HAT

By Charles Mingus

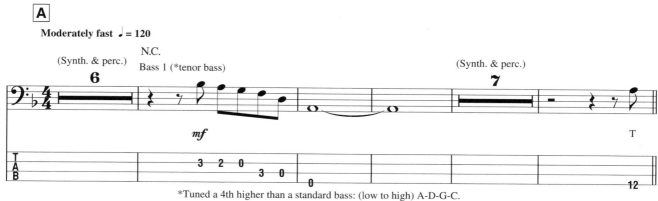

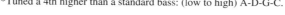

*Tuned a 4th higher than a standard bass: (low to high) A-D-G-C.

**5th string is low B.

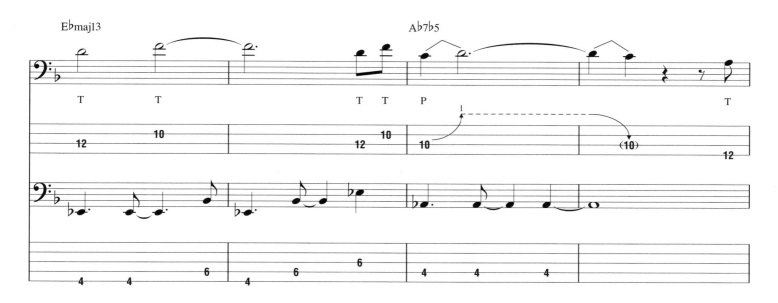

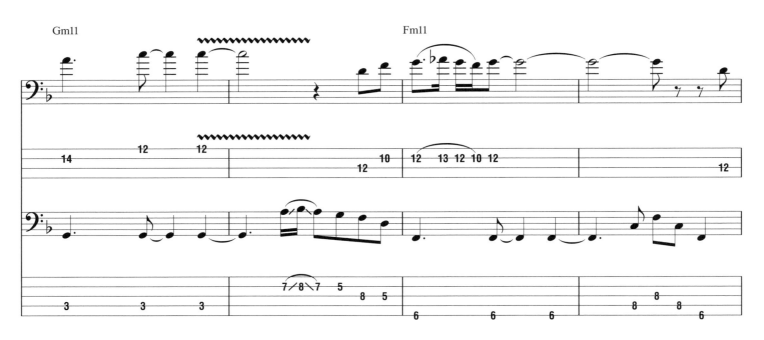

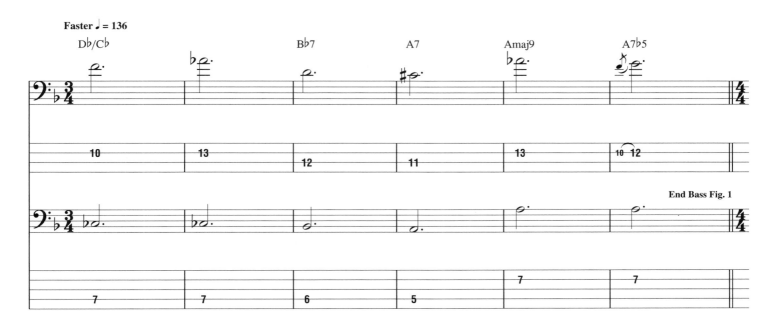

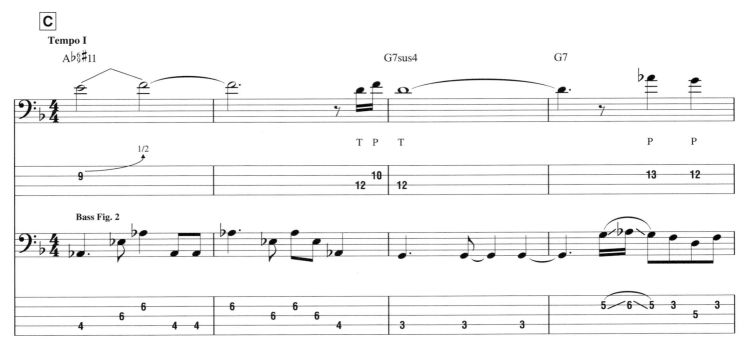

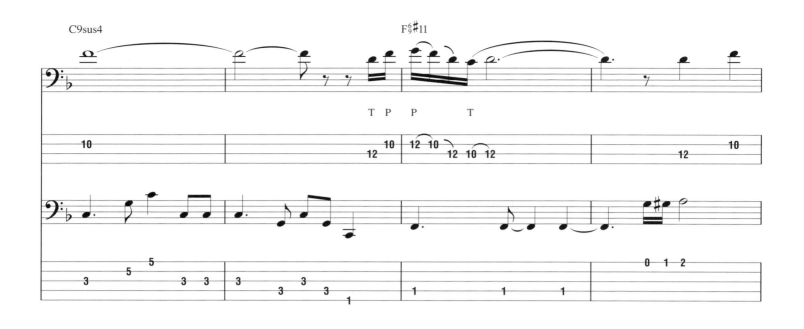

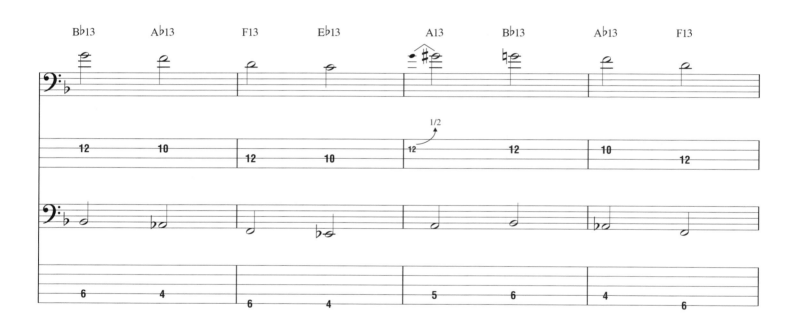

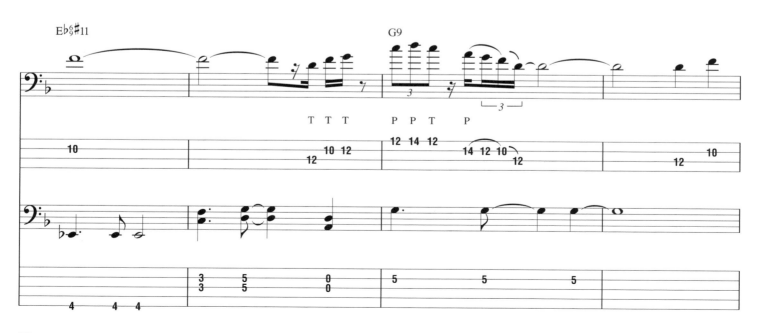

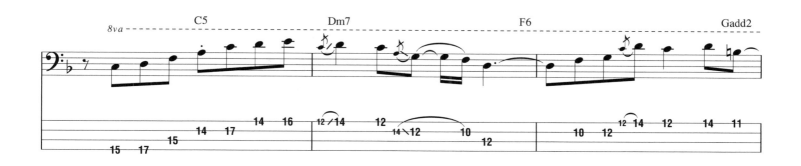

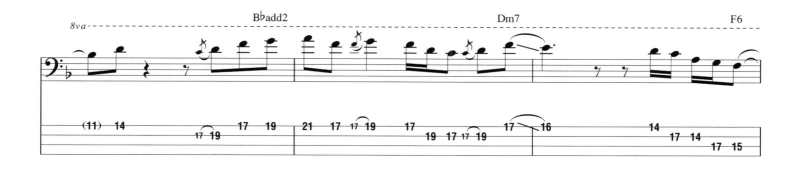

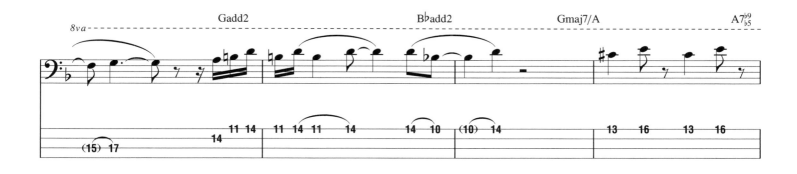

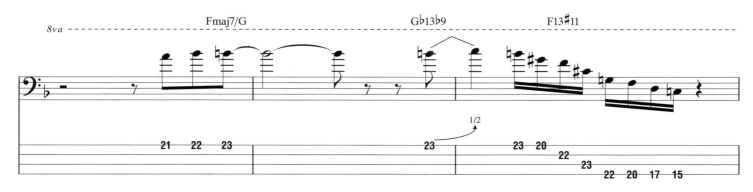

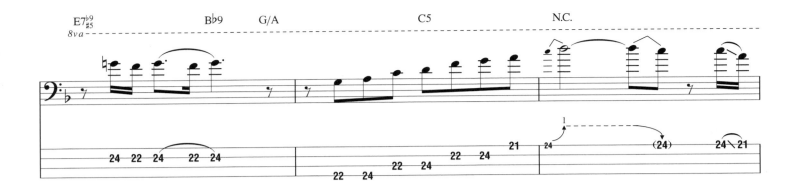

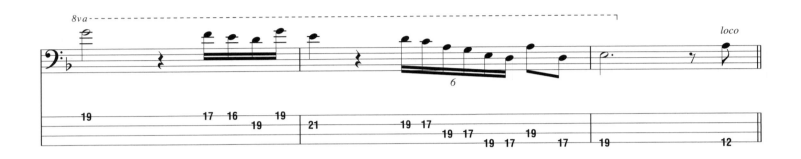

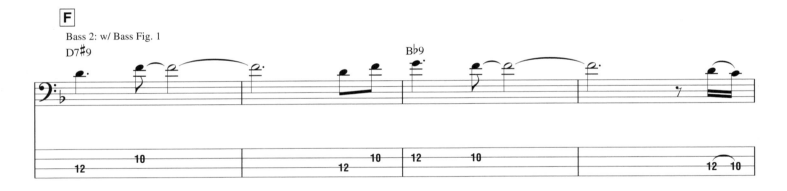

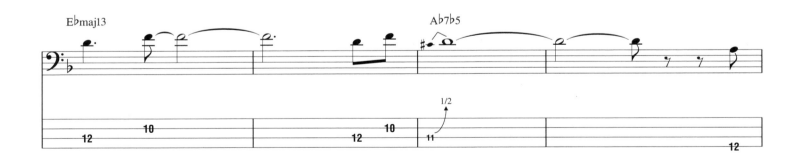

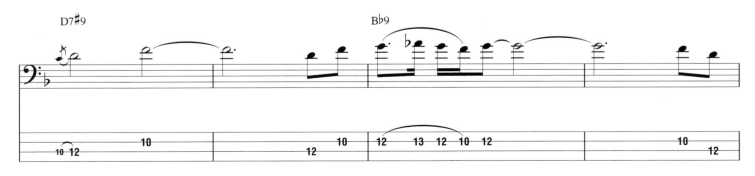

84

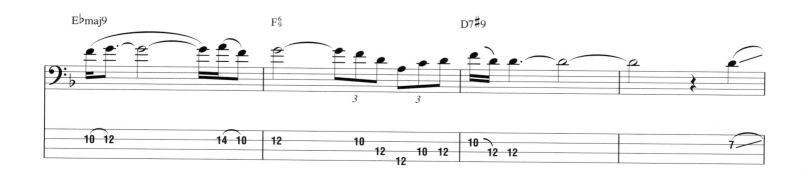

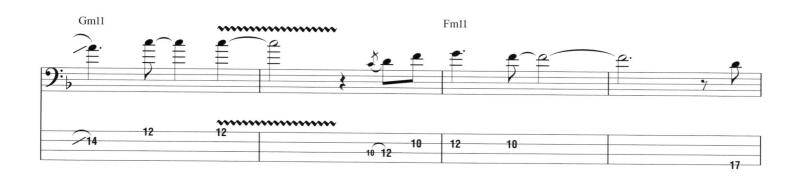

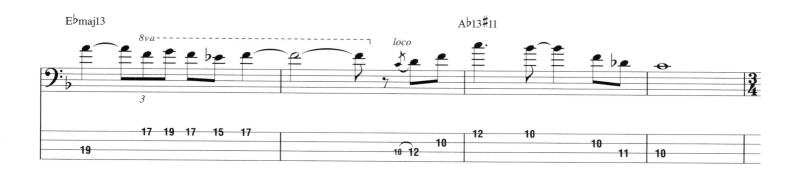

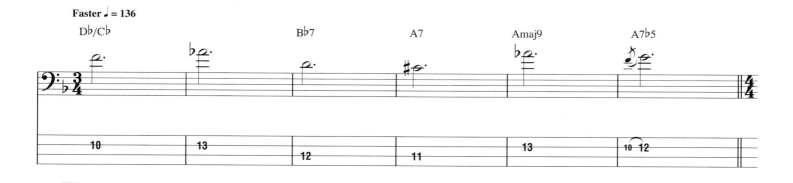

G

Tempo I

Bass 2: w/ Bass Fig. 2

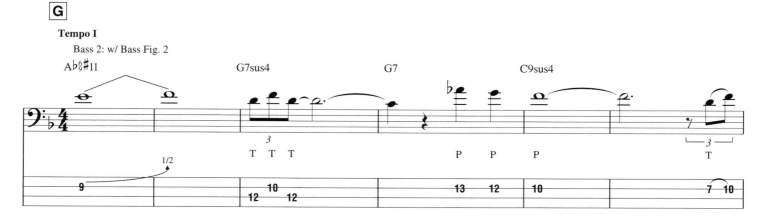

HAIR

Music and Lyrics by
Larry Graham

Intro
Moderately slow Funk ♩ = 79

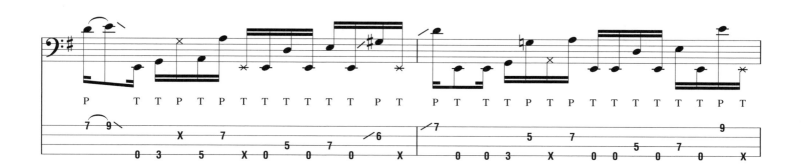

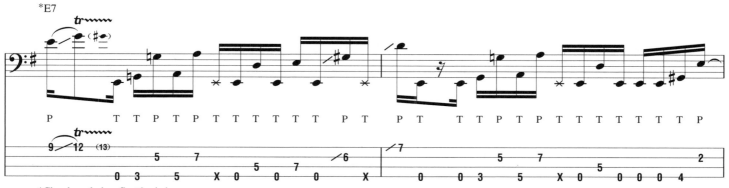

*Chord symbols reflect basic harmony.

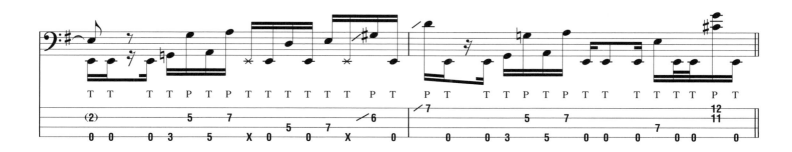

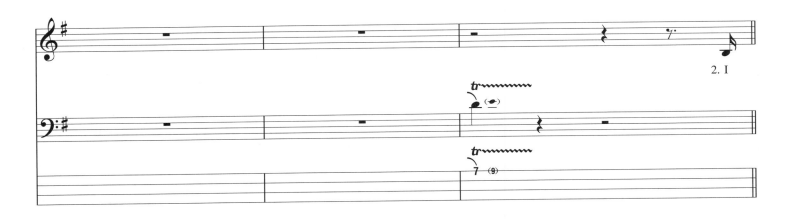

Verse

take two __ words __ like __ "hip" and "square." Hey. The

truth will shine ____ and not your hair. _____ E -

-ven the blind can damn __ well see, huh, what's __

out - side you and in - side me. ___ Down or high, ___

Chorus

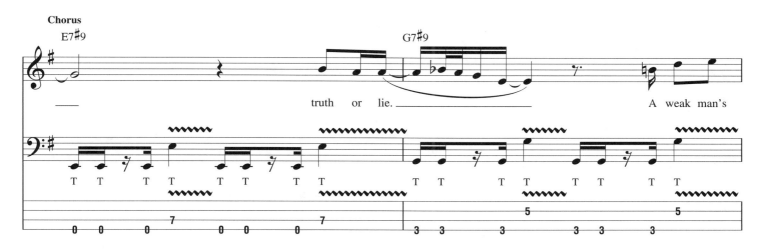

truth or lie. ___ A weak man's

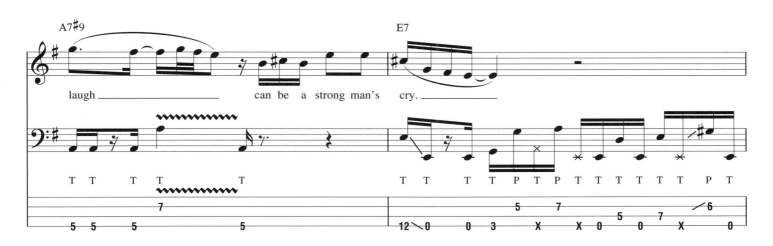

laugh ___ can be a strong man's cry. ___

(Hey, ___ hee. ___ Hey, ___ hee.)

Hey, _____ hee.) _____

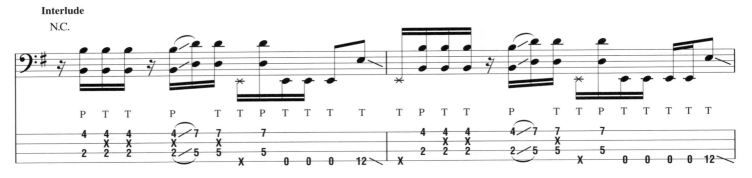

Interlude

N.C.

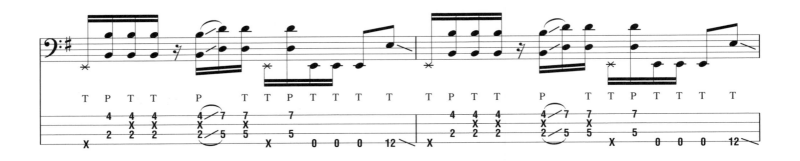

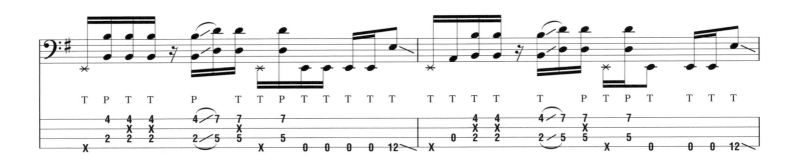

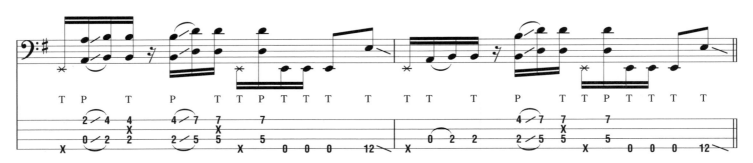

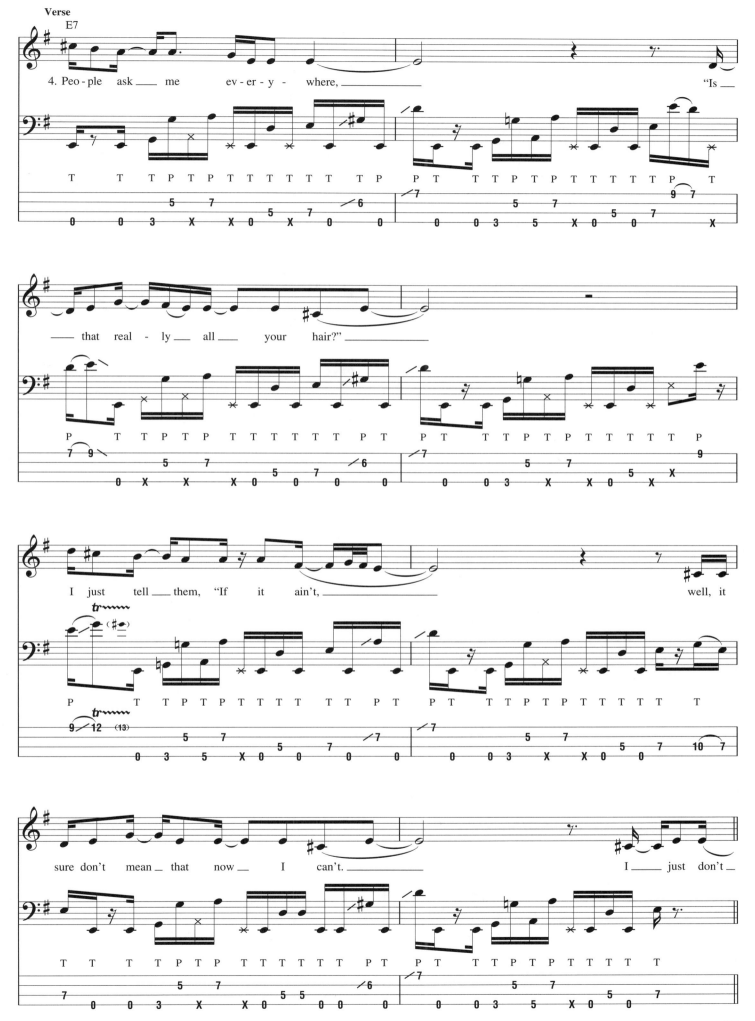

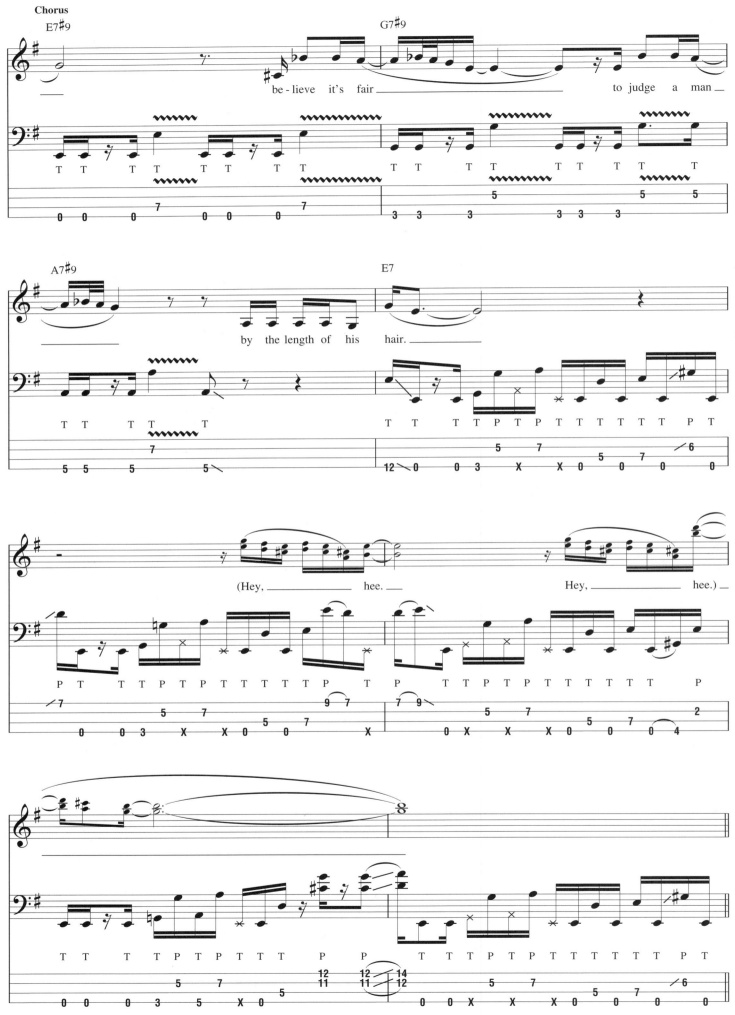

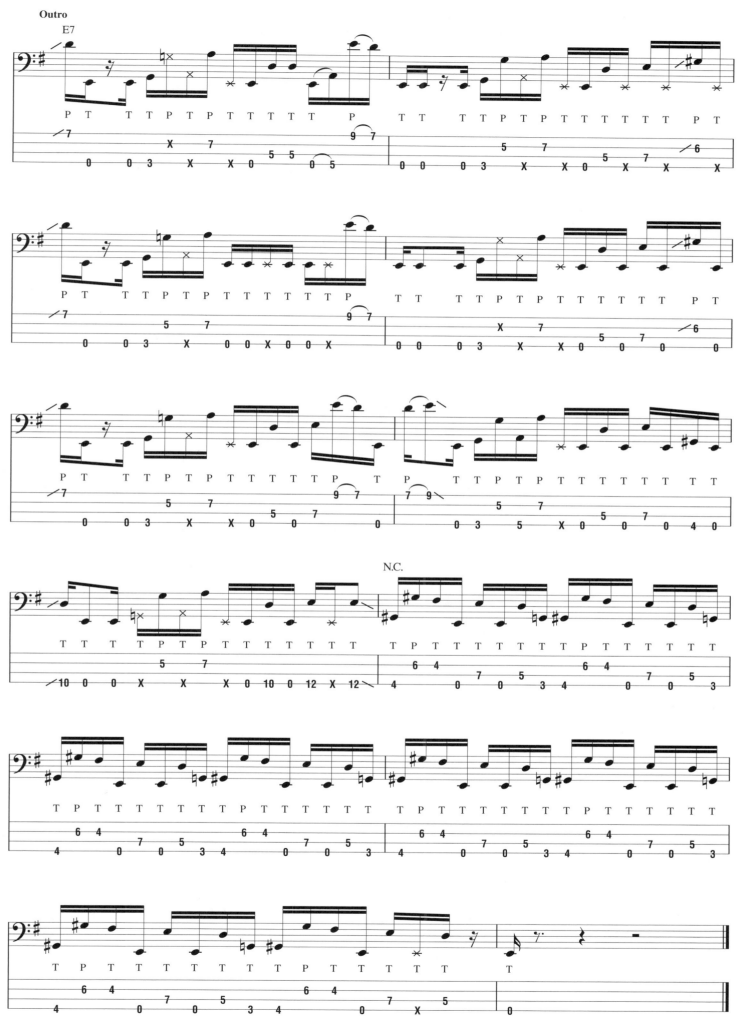

I WANT YOU BACK

Words and Music by
Freddie Perren, Alphonso Mizell,
Berry Gordy and Deke Richards

Moderate Soul ♩ = 100

1. When I had_ you to_ my-self,_ (etc.)
2. Try-ing to live with - out_ your love_ (etc.)

Oh____ ba - by, give__ me one__ more chance....(etc.)

JERRY WAS A RACE CAR DRIVER

Music by Primus
Lyrics by Claypool

* Bass tuning:
(low to high) B–E–A–D–G–C

Intro
Moderate Rock ♩ = 128
N.C.

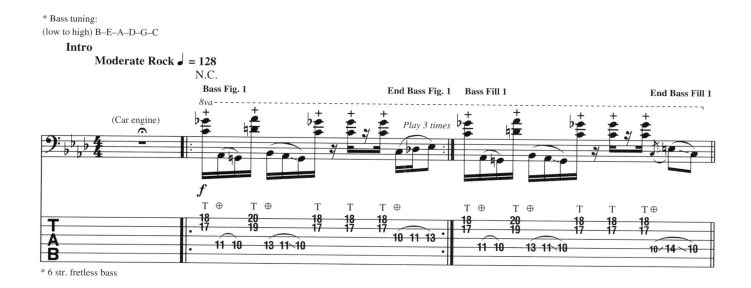

* 6 str. fretless bass

Verse

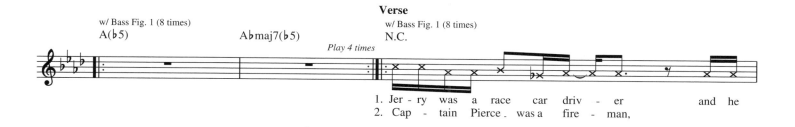

w/ Bass Fig. 1 (8 times)
A(♭5)   A♭maj7(♭5)
Play 4 times
w/ Bass Fig. 1 (8 times)
N.C.

1. Jer - ry was a race car driv - er and he
2. Cap - tain Pierce was a fire - man,

drove so god - damned fast. He nev - er did win no check - ered flags, but he
Rich - mond en - gine num - ber three. I'll be a wealth - y man when I get that dime for all the

nev - er did come in last. Jer - ry was a race car driv - er. He'd say,
things that man had taught to me. Cap - tain Pierce was a strong man,

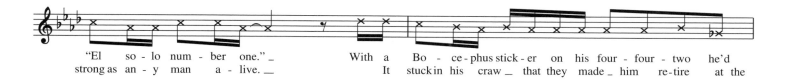

"El so - lo num - ber one." With a Bo - ce - phus stick - er on his four - four - two he'd
strong as an - y man a - live. It stuck in his craw that they made him re - tire at the

101

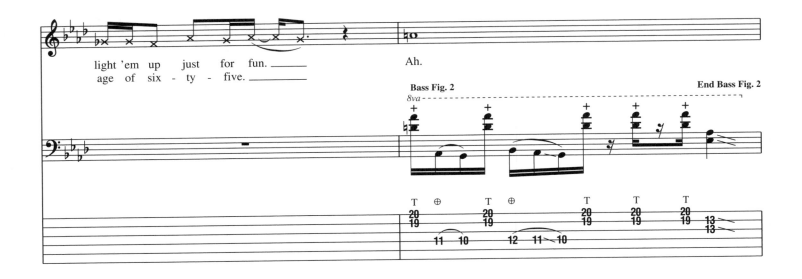

light 'em up   just   for   fun. _____   Ah.
age of   six - ty - five. _____

Bass Fig. 2   **End Bass Fig. 2**

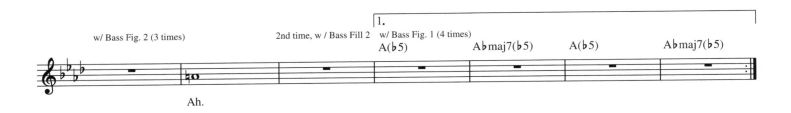

w/ Bass Fig. 2 (3 times)   2nd time, w / Bass Fill 2   w/ Bass Fig. 1 (4 times)

1.

A(♭5)   A♭maj7(♭5)   A(♭5)   A♭maj7(♭5)

Ah.

2.
w/ Bass Fig. 1 (3 times)
A(♭5)   A♭maj7(♭5)   A(♭5)

Go!

A♭maj7(♭5)   E5   *Play 3 times*

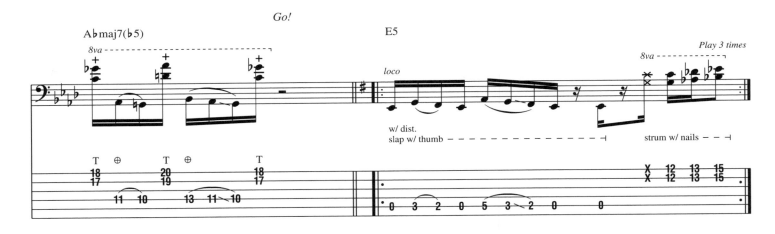

w/ dist.
slap w/ thumb — — — — — — — — — —   strum w/ nails — — —

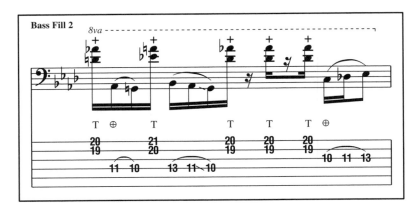

Bass Fill 2

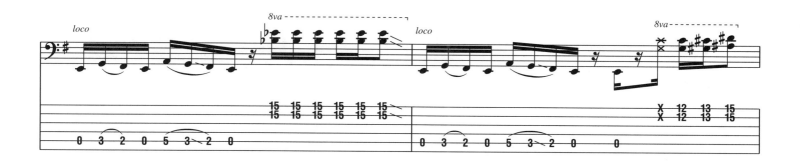

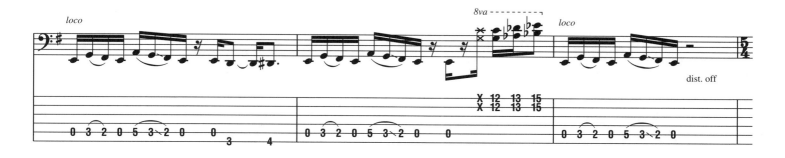

Dog will hunt.

Guitar Solo

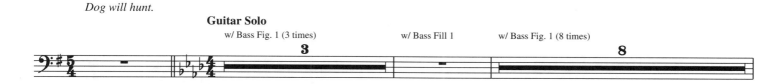

Verse

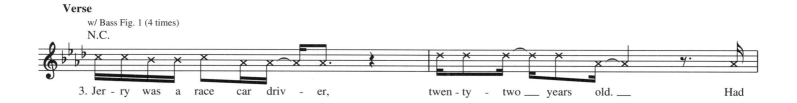

Outro

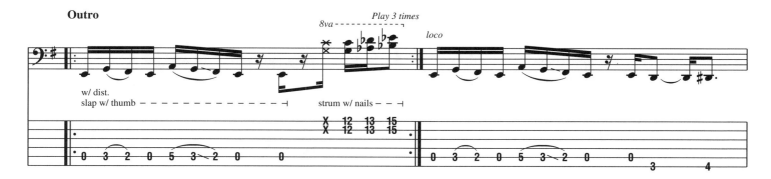

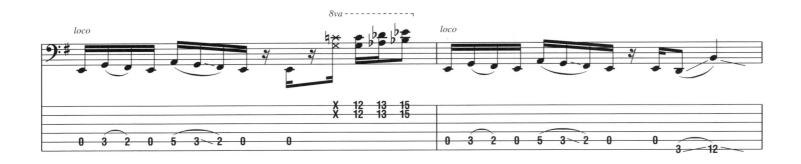

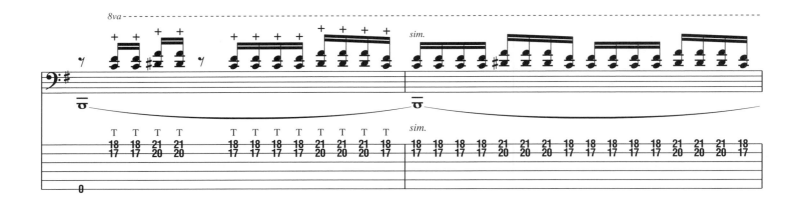

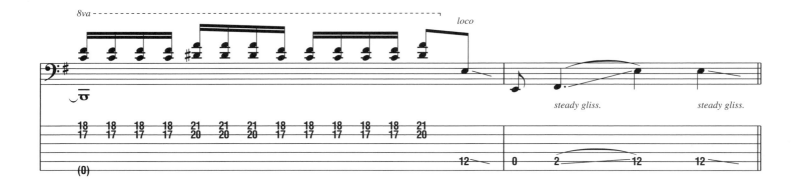

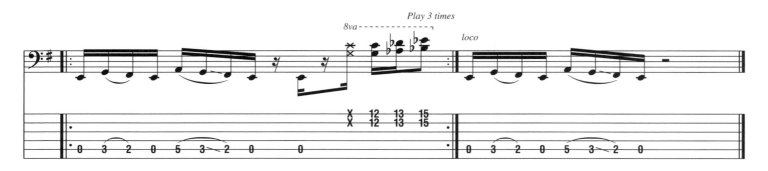

LOST WITHOUT U

Words and Music by
Robin Thicke and Sean Hurley

*Play all chords as two-handed taps. RH taps top two notes while LH taps bottom note.

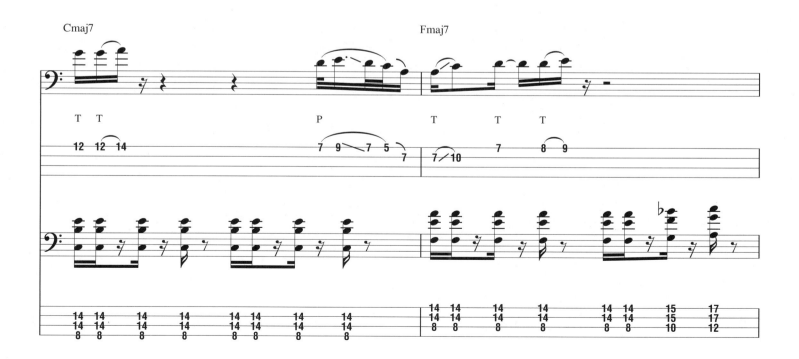

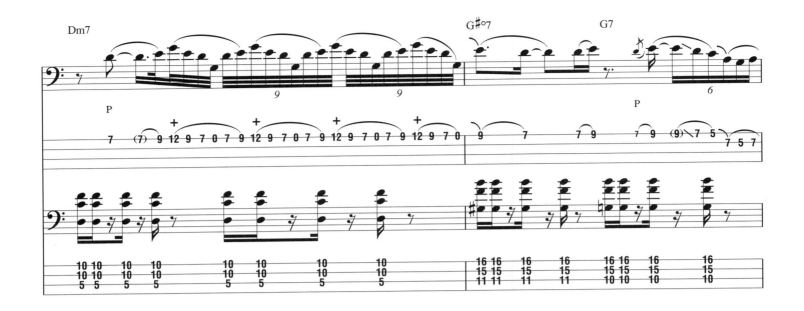

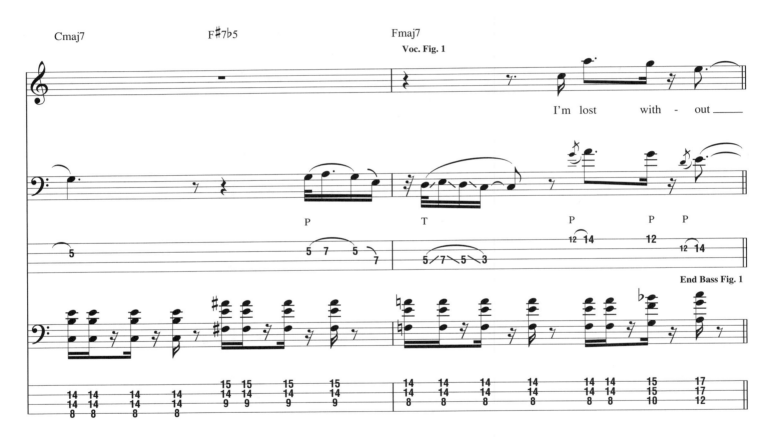

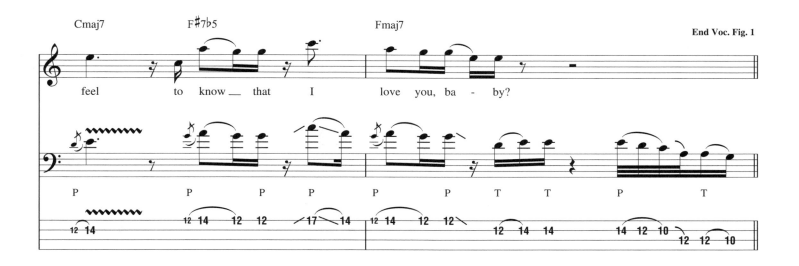

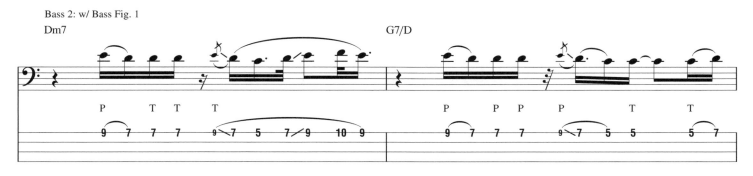

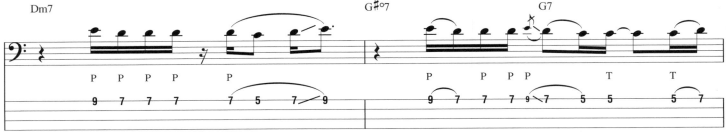

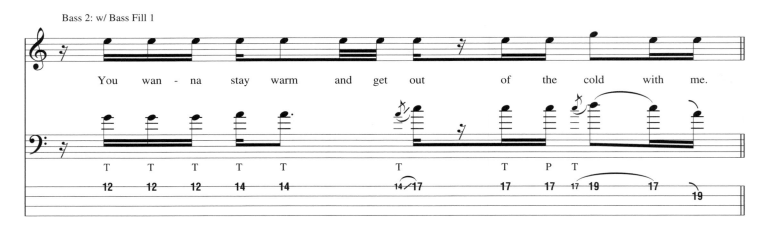

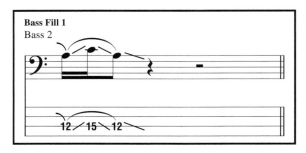

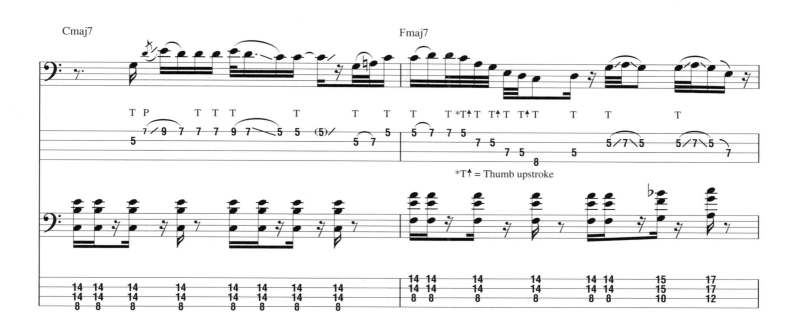

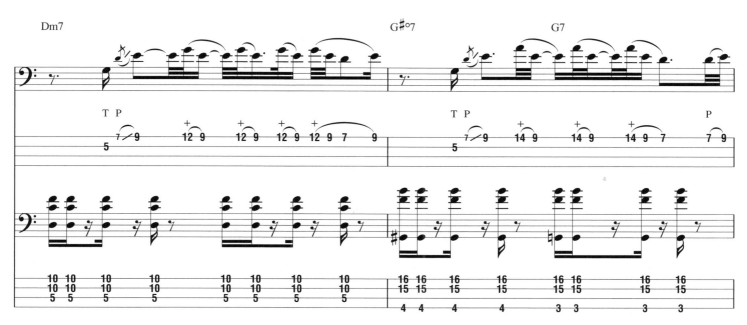

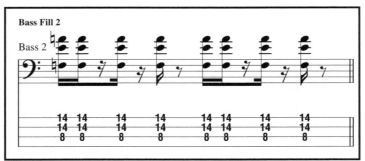

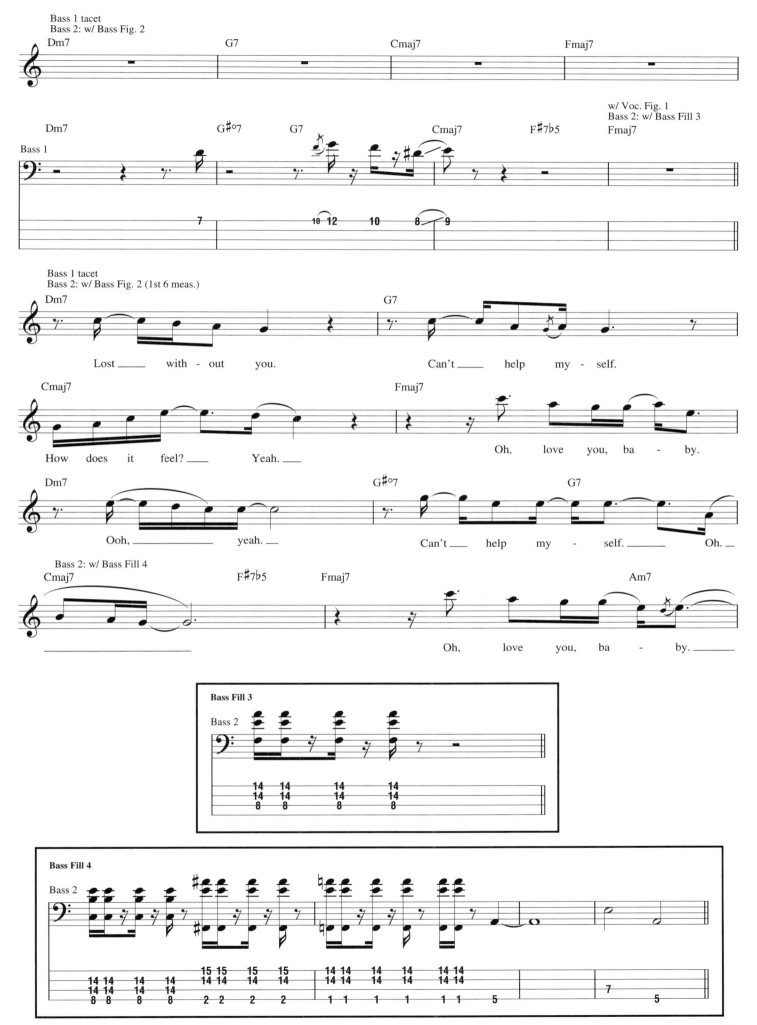

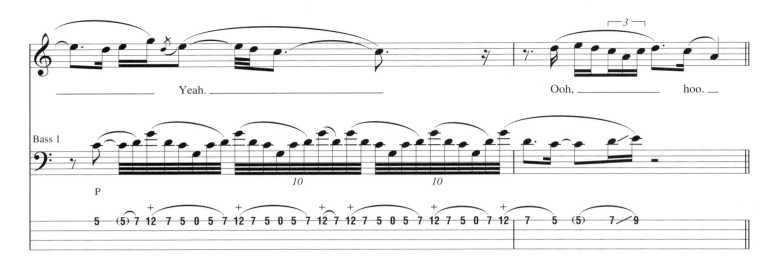

Yeah.   Ooh,   hoo.

Bass 2: w/ Bass Fig. 1

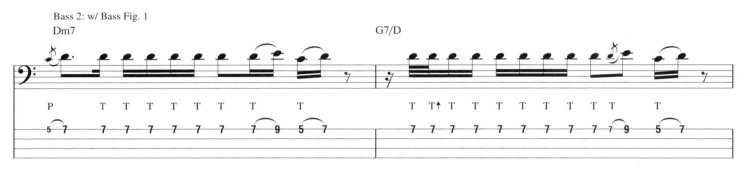

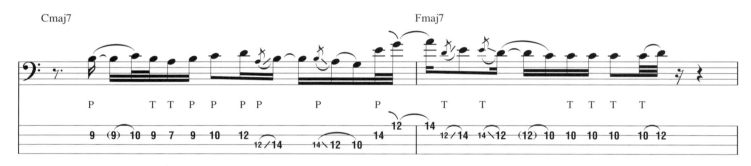

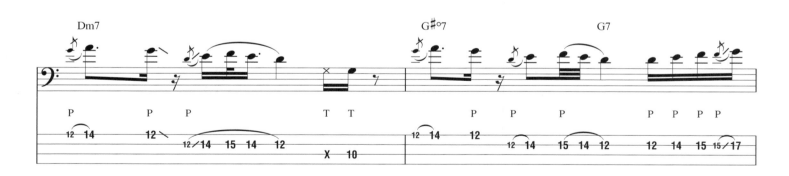

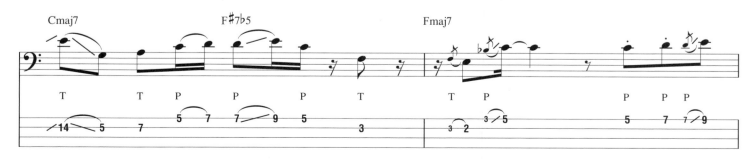

Bass 2: w/*Bass Fig. 3 (till end)

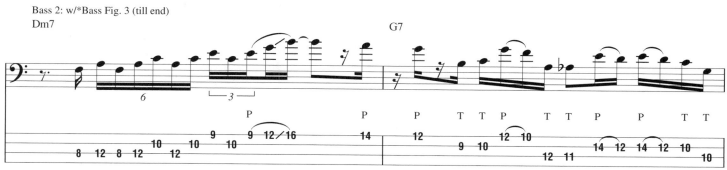

*Bass Fig. 3 consists of Bass Fig. 2 plus Bass Fill 2.

w/ Voc. Fig. 2

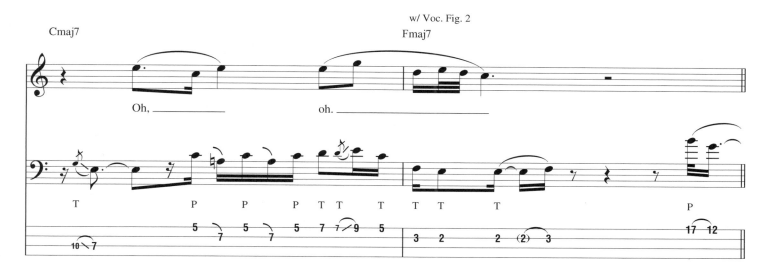

Oh, _____ oh.

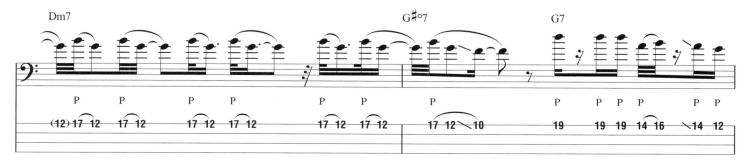

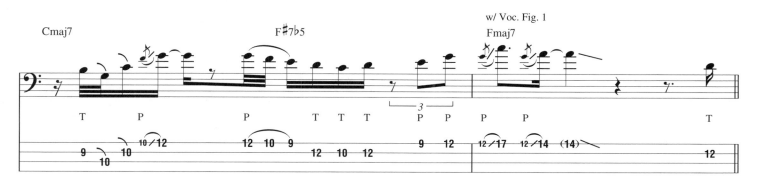

w/ Voc. Fig. 1

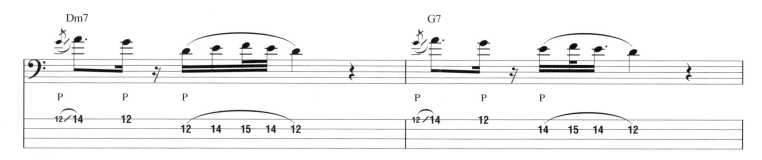

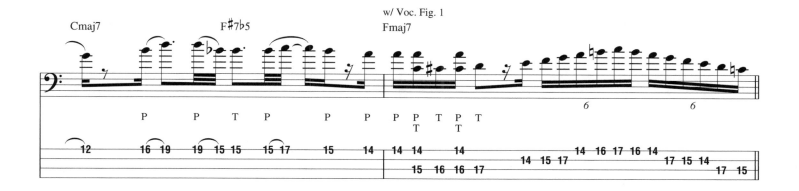

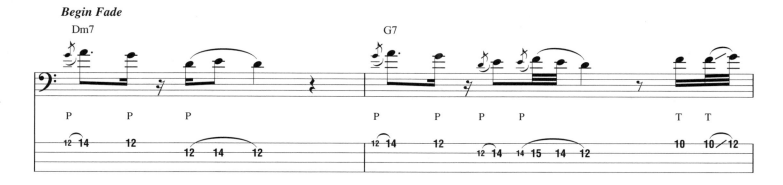

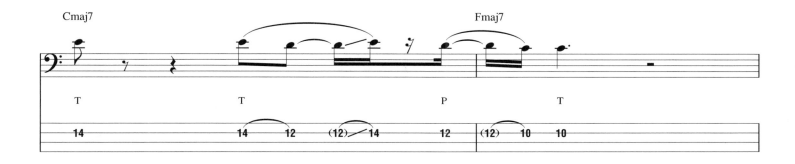

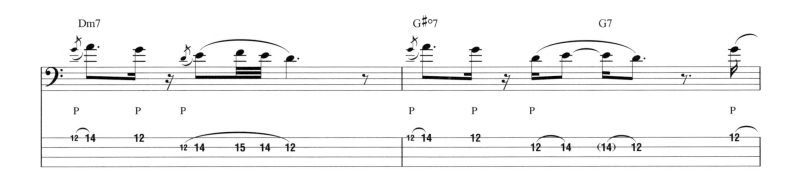

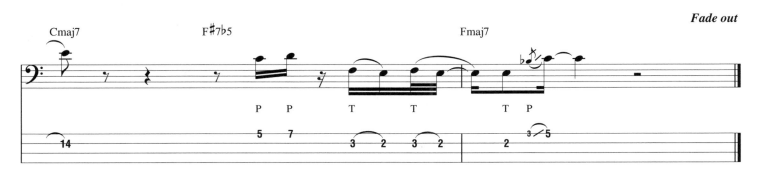

ME AND MY BASS GUITAR

Written by
Victor Wooten

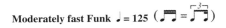

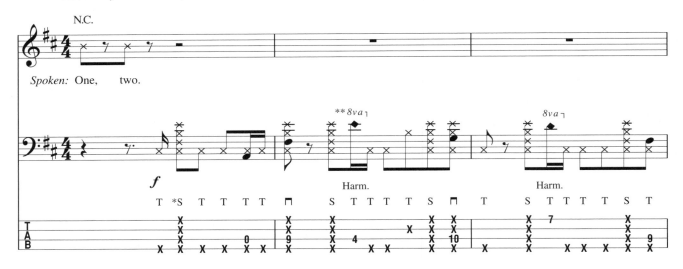

*S = Slap all four right-hand fingers against the indicated string(s).

**8va refers to harmonics only, throughout.

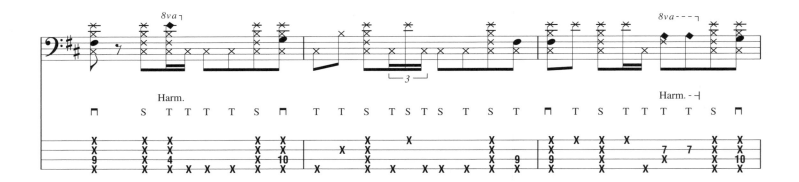

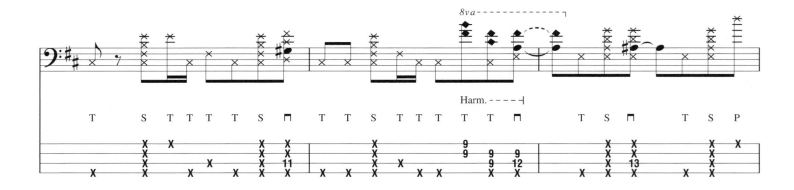

*L = left-hand tap; R = right-hand tap. The numbers 1, 2, 3, and 4 indicate the index, middle, ring, and little fingers, respectively (for each hand).

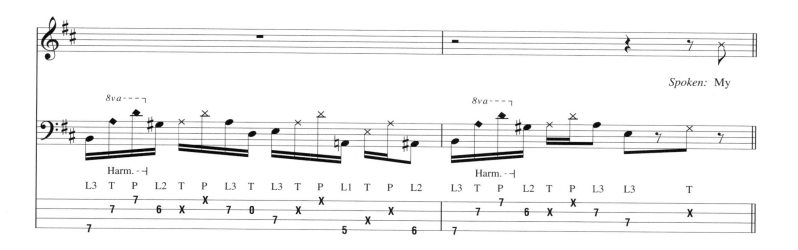

Spoken: My

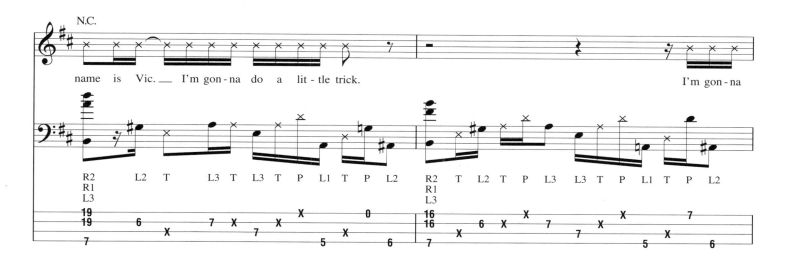

name is Vic. __ I'm gon-na do a lit-tle trick.

I'm gon-na

play my bass __ with-out us-in' a pick. __

Trav-el

'round the world ___ and back a - gain. ___   I just

takin' my bass out for a spin, ___   if ya know what I'm say - in'.

And if you're ev - er look - in' for me,   I don't go too far.

Cuz if ya real - ly wan - na find me, ___   ya know where I are. With

me and my bass gui - tar.

*T↑ = Thumb upstroke

Uh, you say it.

Me and my bass gui - tar. That's right.

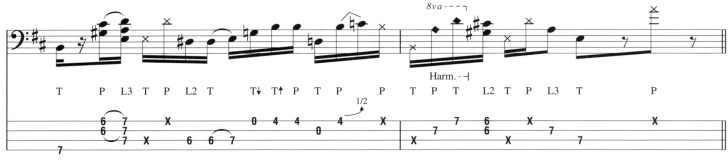

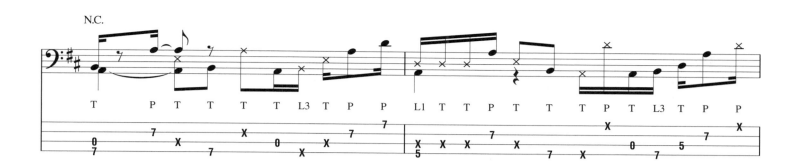

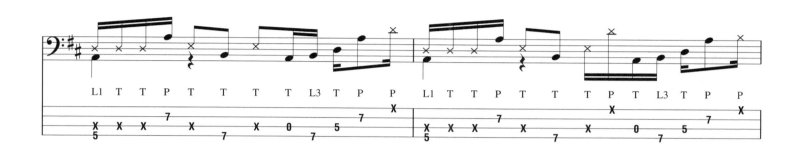

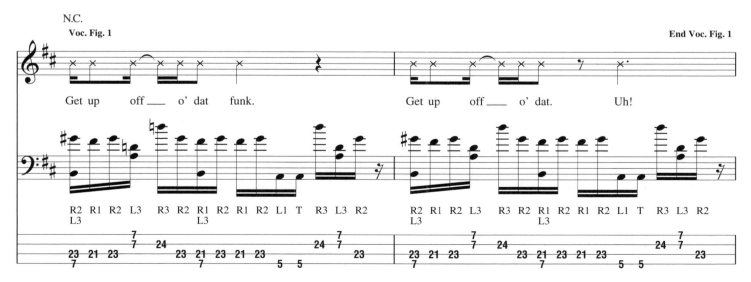

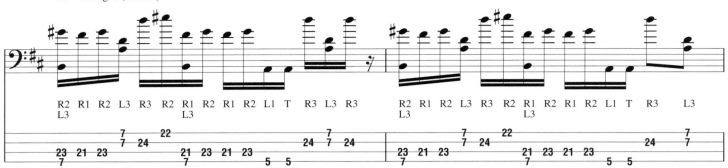

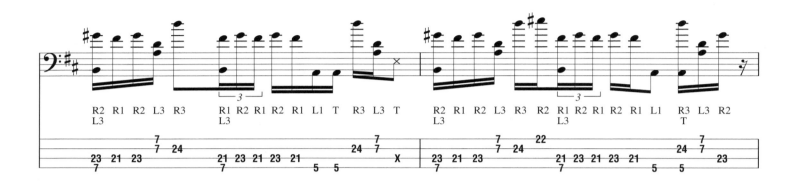

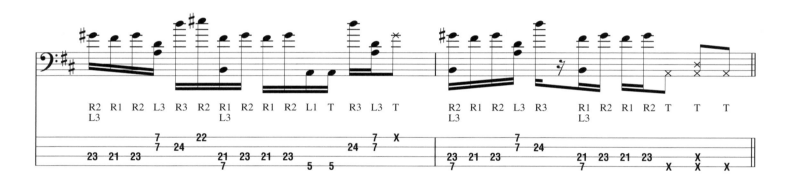

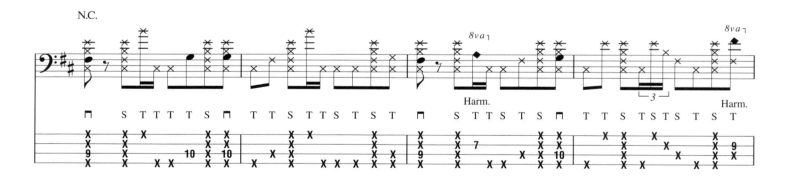

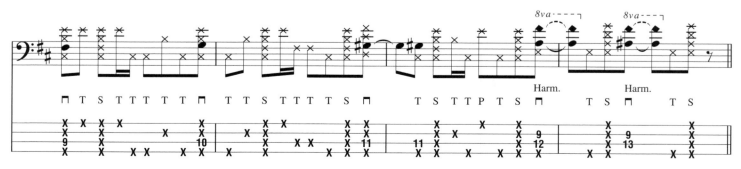

124

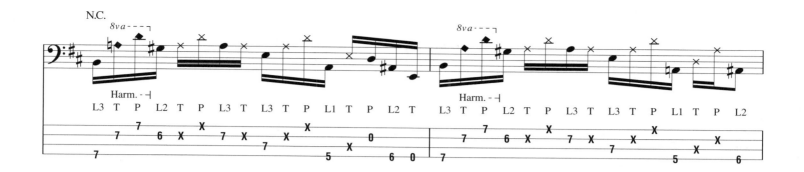

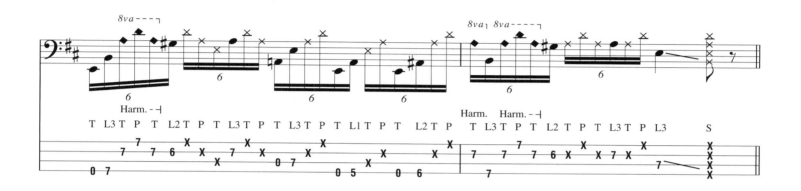

Me and my bass gui - tar.

Uh, that's

right. Just my four strings _____ and me. _____

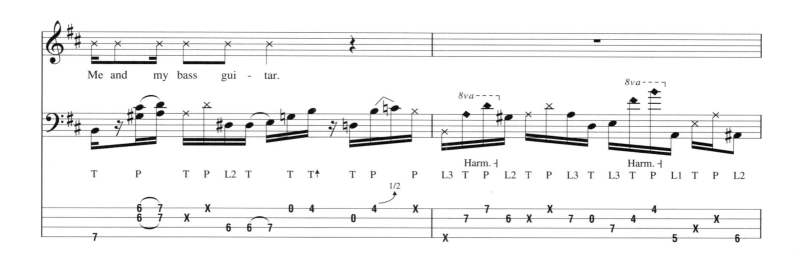

Me and my bass gui - tar.

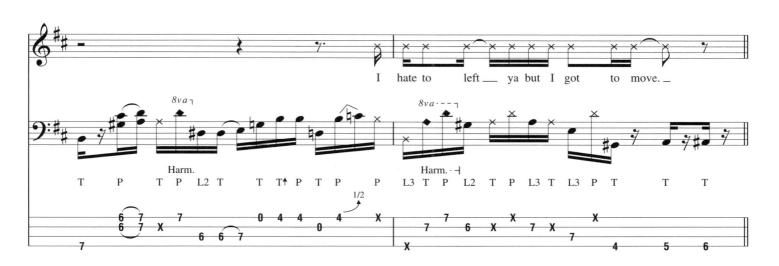

I hate to left __ ya but I got to move. __

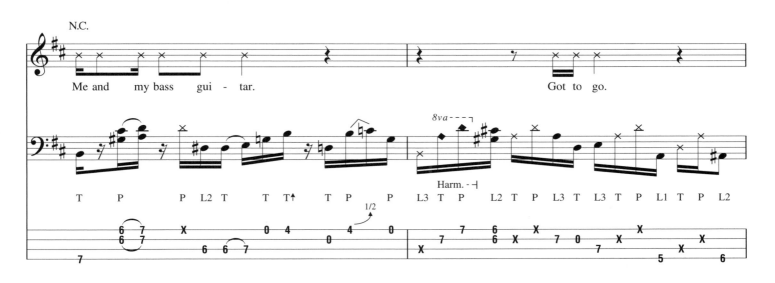

N.C.

Me and my bass gui - tar.

Got to go.

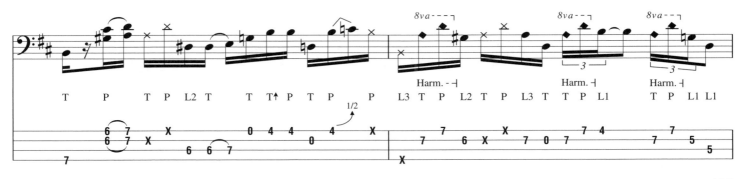

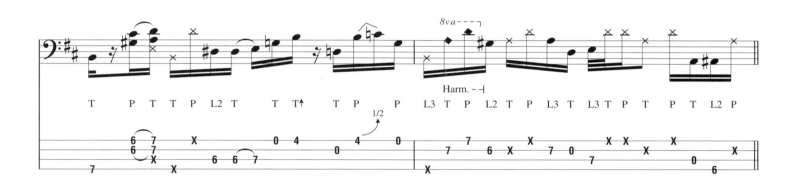

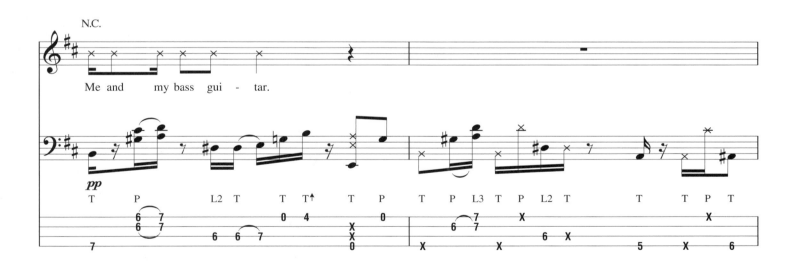

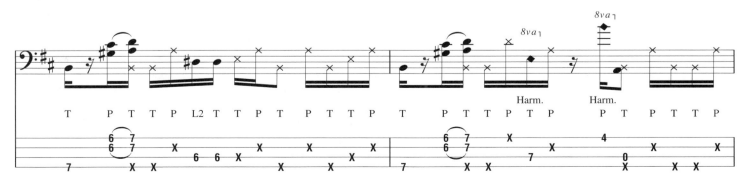

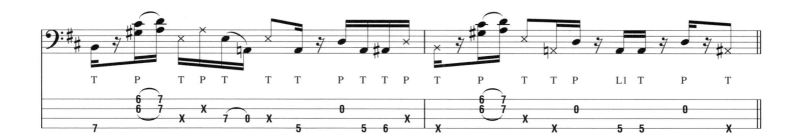

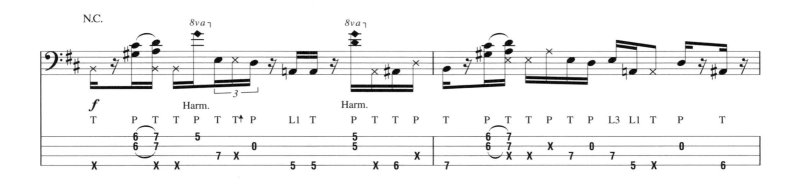

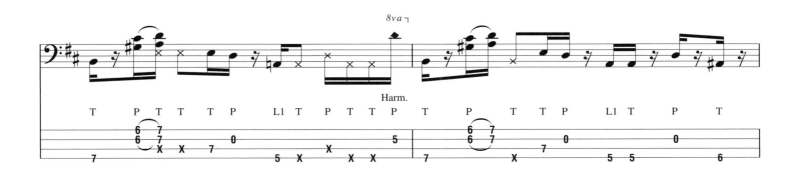

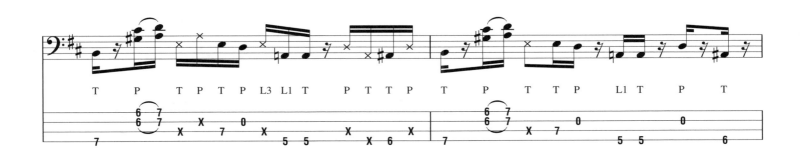

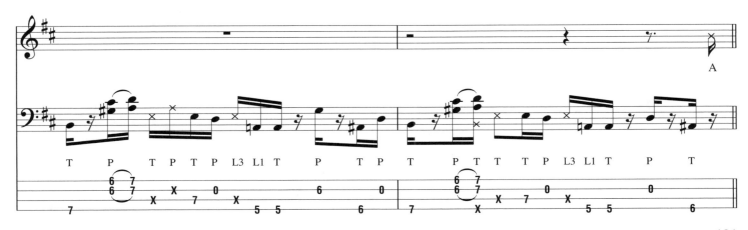

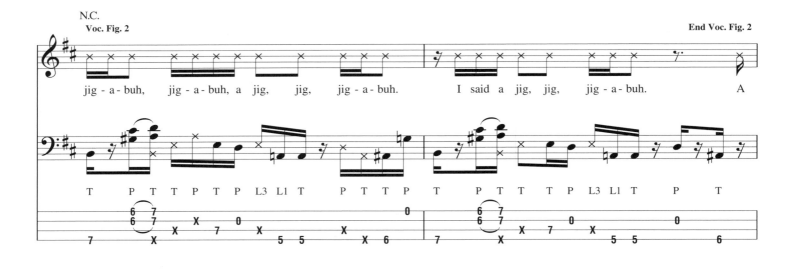

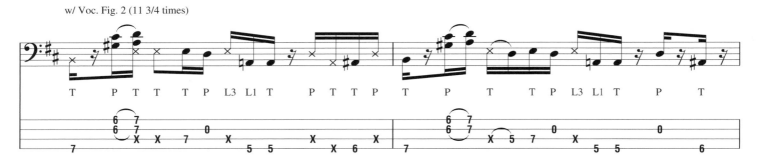

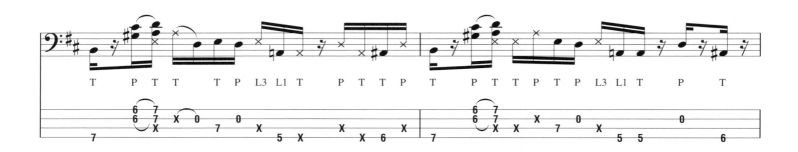

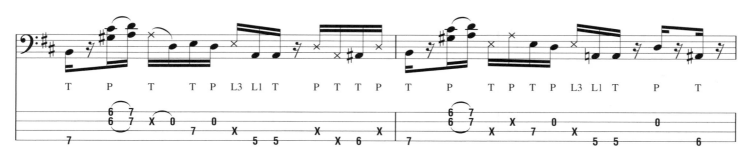

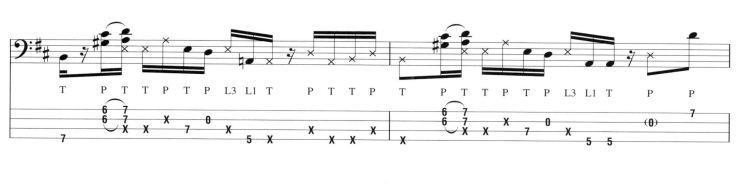

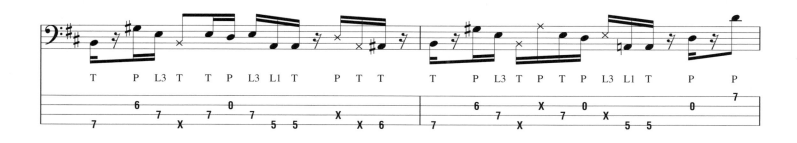

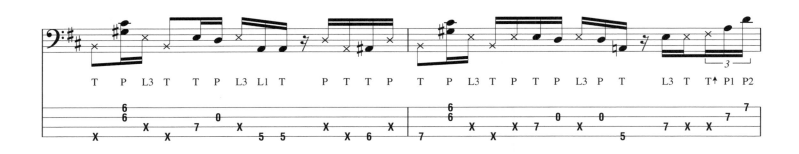

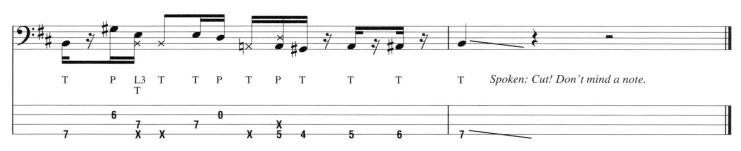

Spoken: Cut! Don't mind a note.

134

NV43345

Music by Billy Sheehan

*Tap G w/1st fin. of pick hand;
tap A w/3rd fin. of pick hand.

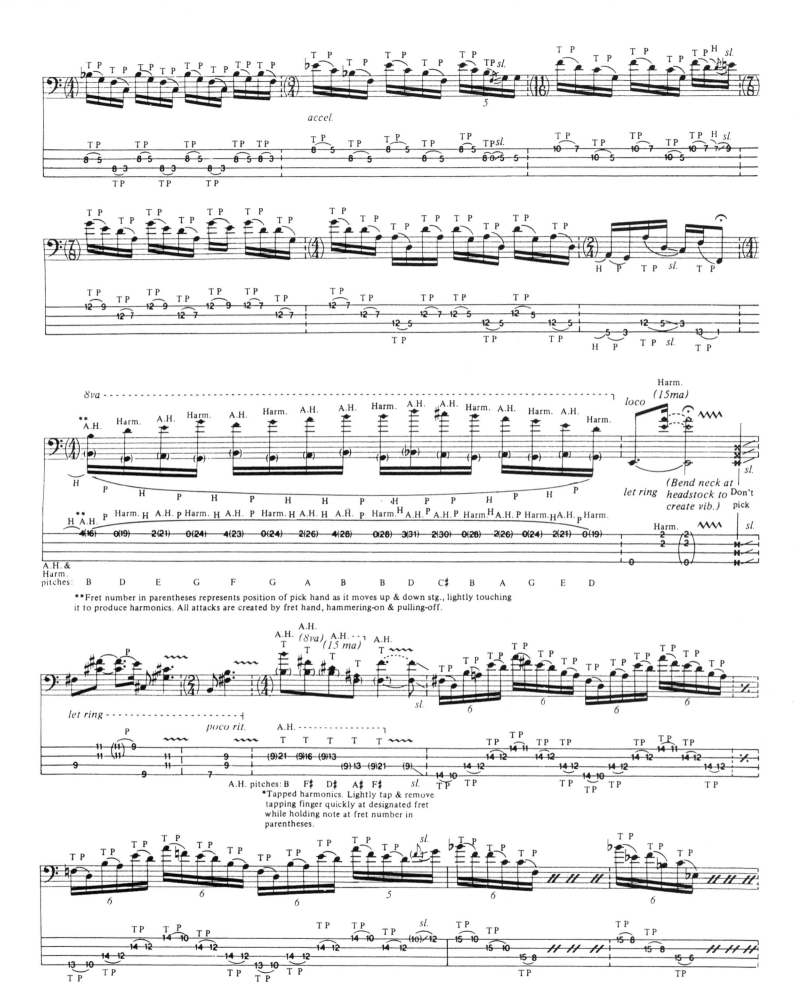

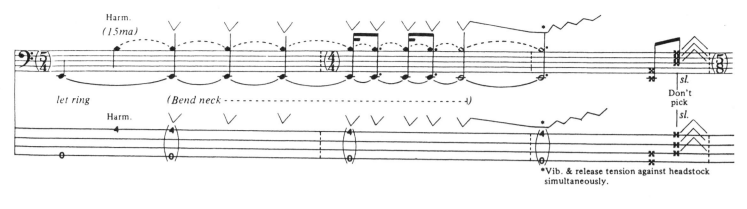

Vib. & release tension against headstock simultaneously.

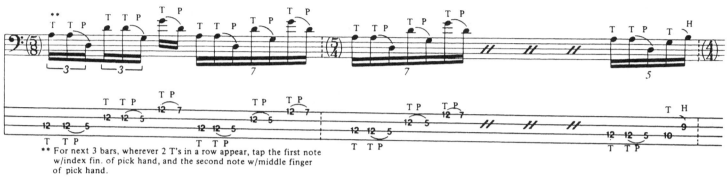

** For next 3 bars, wherever 2 T's in a row appear, tap the first note w/index fin. of pick hand, and the second note w/middle finger of pick hand.

† For next 3 bars, wherever 2 T's in a row appear, tap both w/index fin. of pick hand.

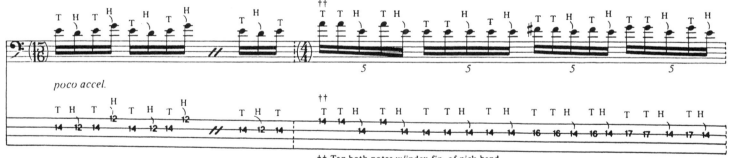

†† Tap both notes w/index fin. of pick hand.

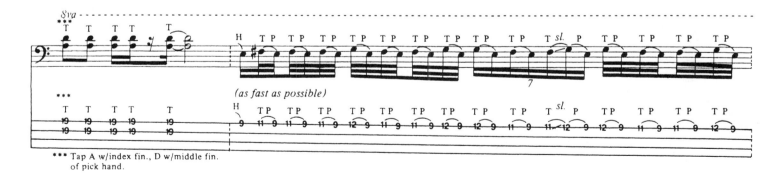

*** Tap A w/index fin., D w/middle fin. of pick hand.

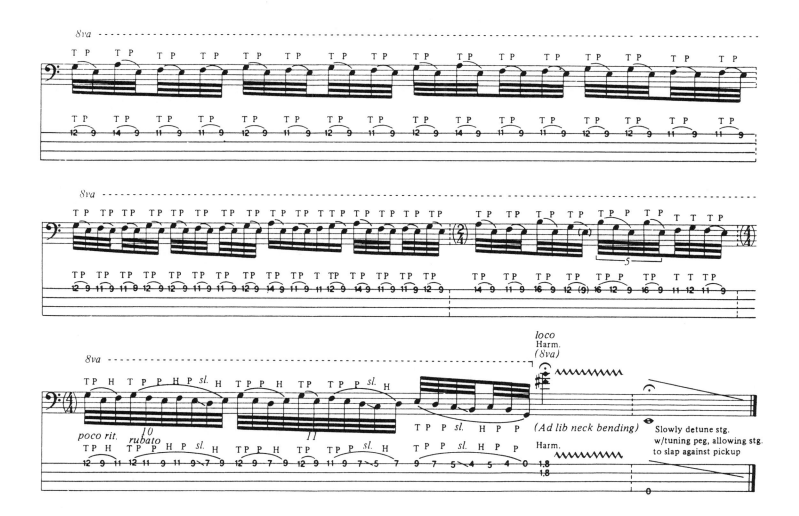

ROUNDABOUT

Words and Music by
Jon Anderson and Steve Howe

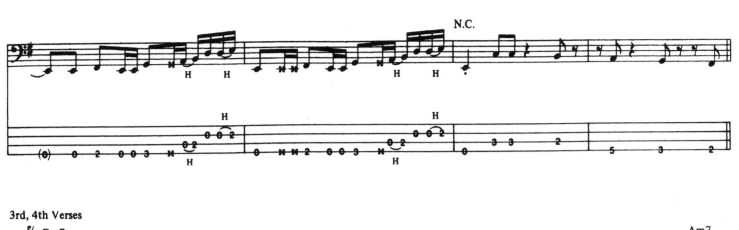

3rd, 4th Verses

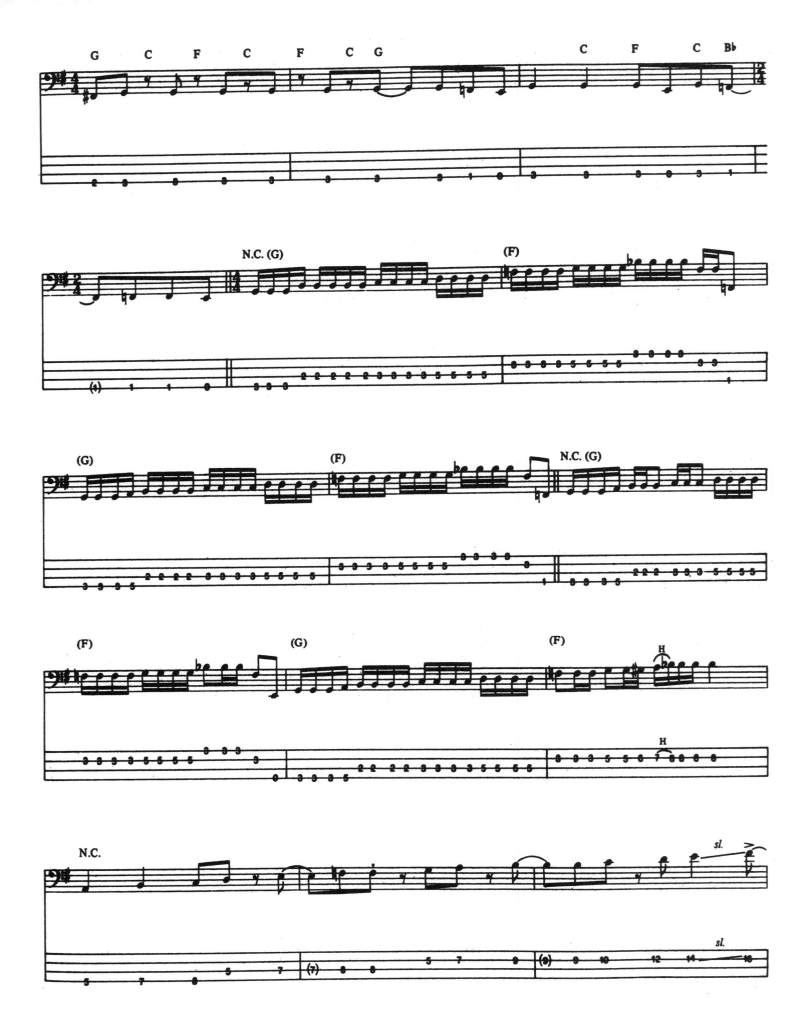

147

SCHOOL DAYS

By Stanley Clarke

* Key signature denotes A Mixolydian.

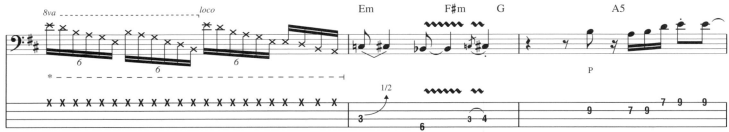

* Slide down string in specific rhythm, pitches are approx.

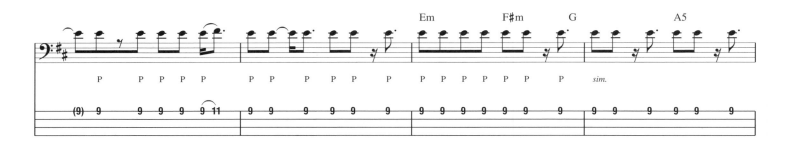

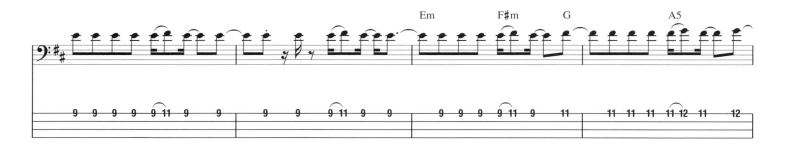

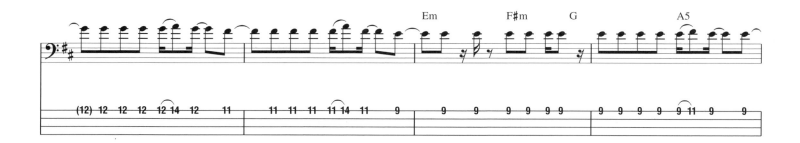

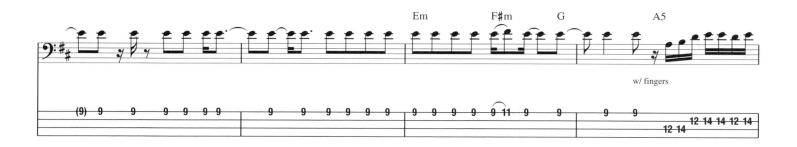

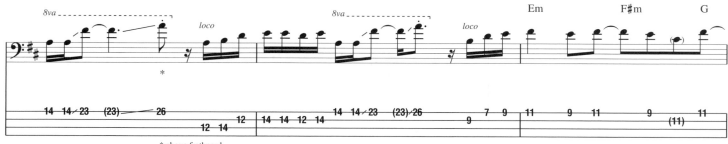

* above fretboard

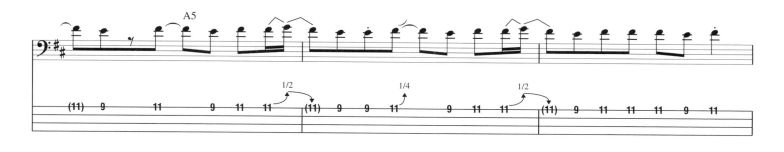

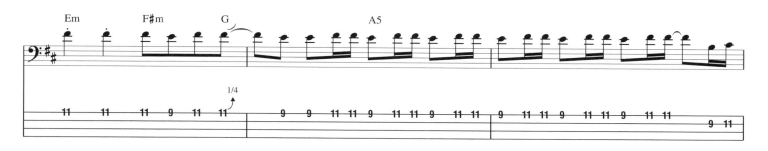

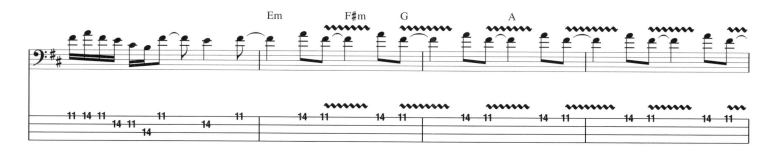

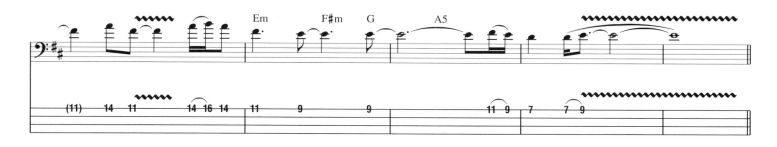

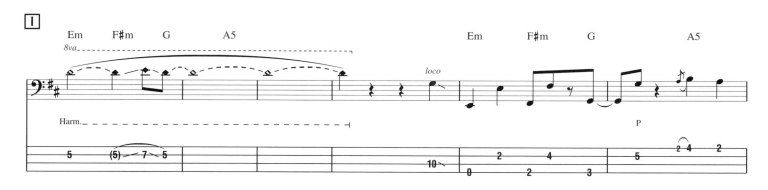

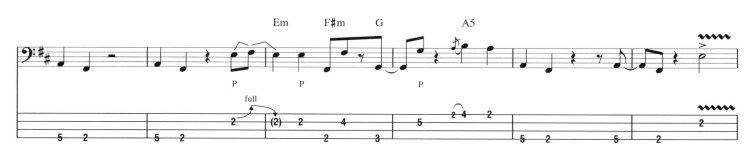

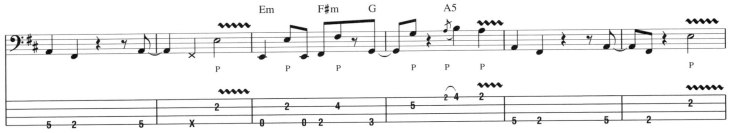

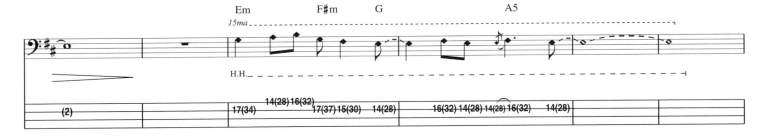

Bass: w/ Bass Fig. 2, 2 times, simile

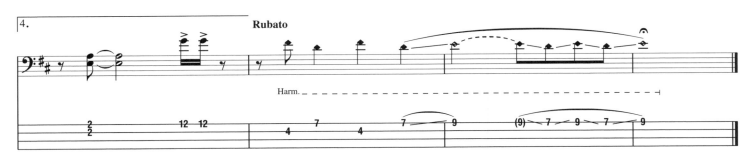

SHY BOY

Words and Music by
Billy Sheehan

Chorus

Shy boy,— shy——— boy, *etc.*

158

SLEIGH RIDE

By Leroy Anderson

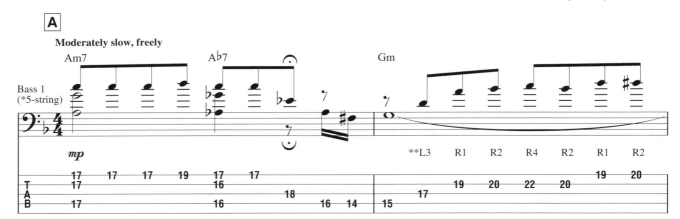

*5th string is low B.

**L = left-hand tap; R = right-hand tap. The numbers 1, 2, 3, and 4 indicate the index, middle, ring, and little fingers, respectively (for each hand).

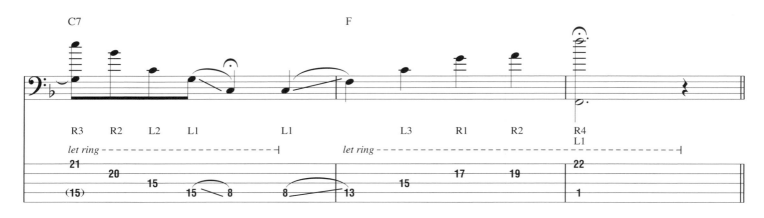

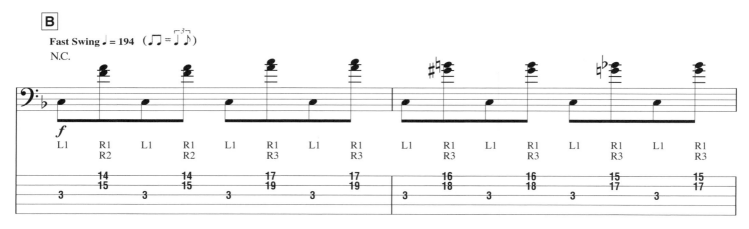

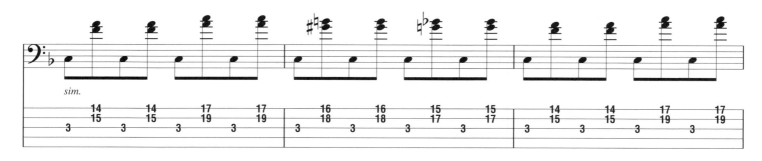

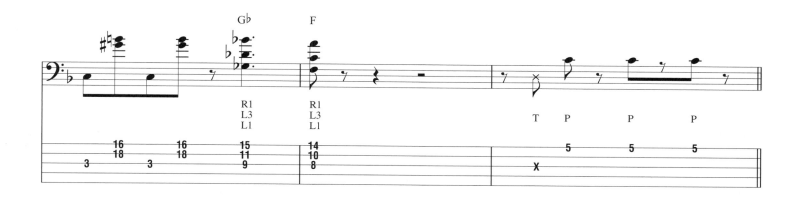

*Chord symbols reflect basic harmony.

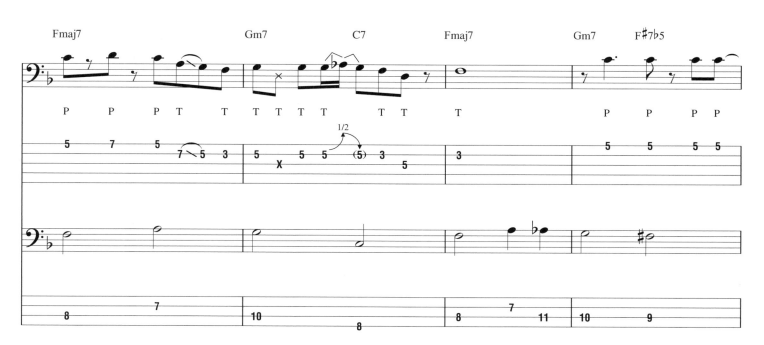

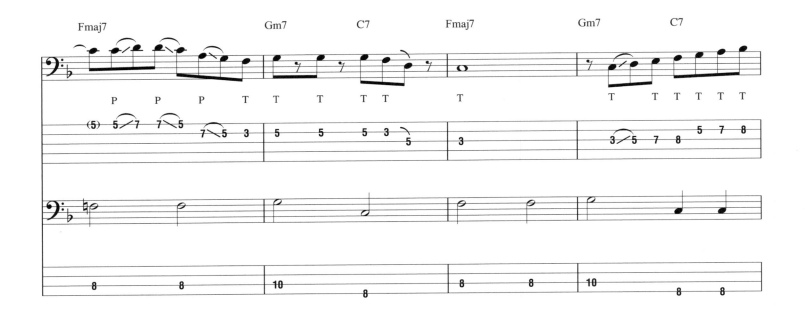

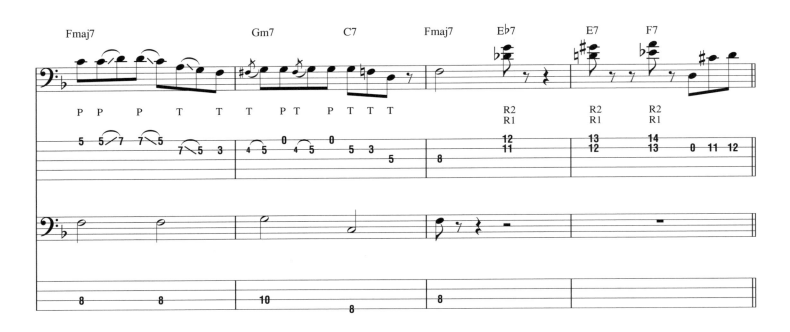

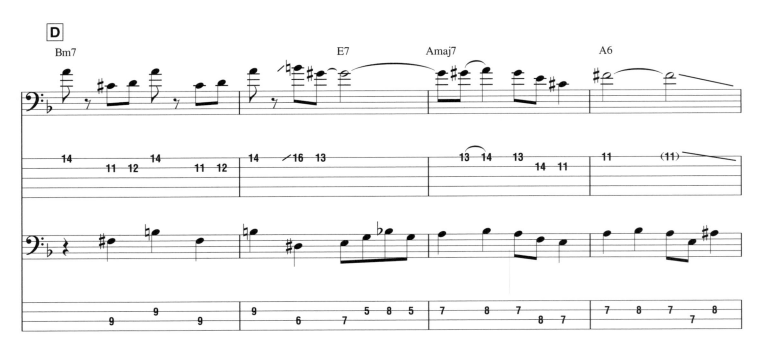

162

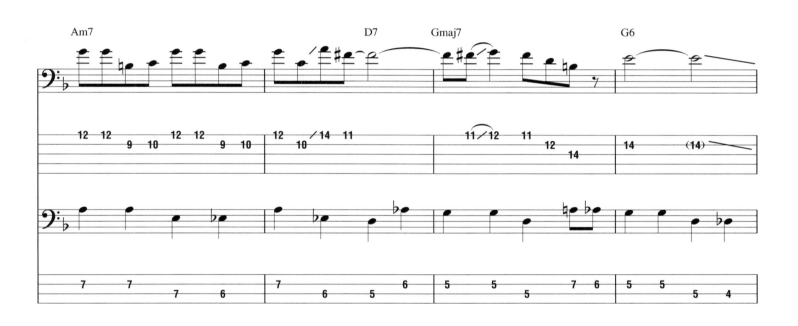

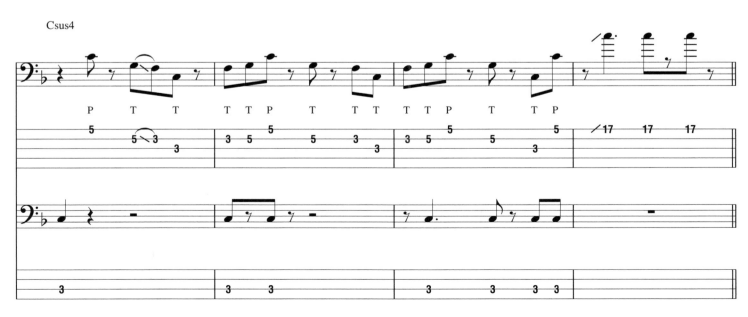

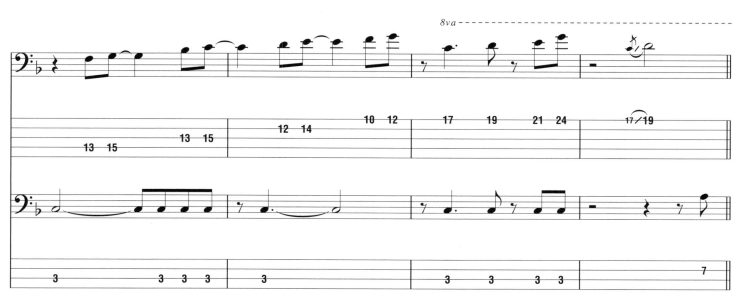

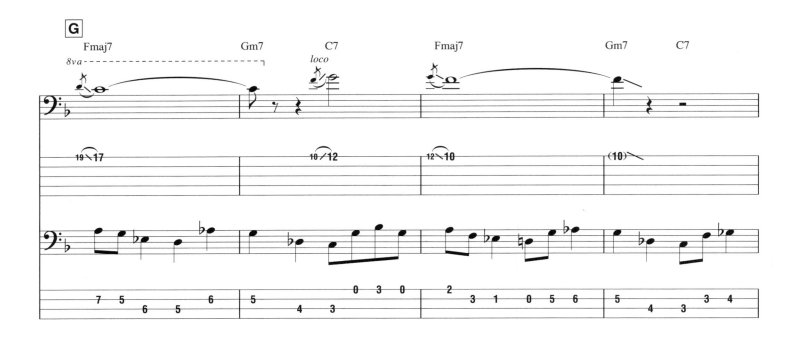

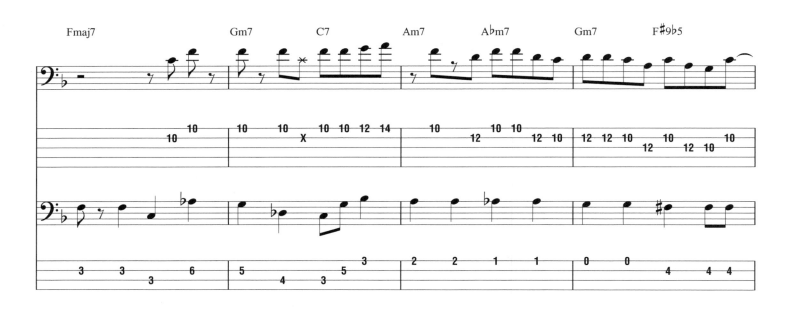

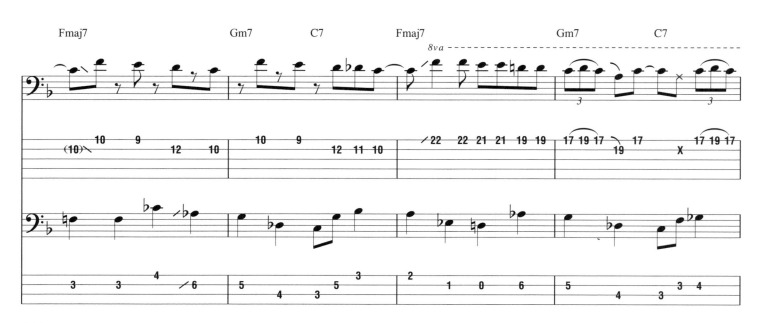

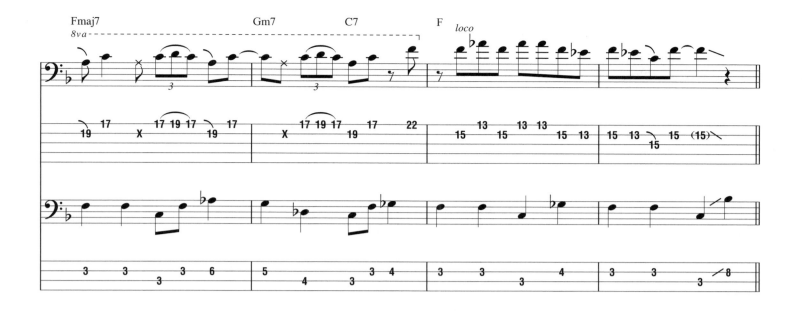

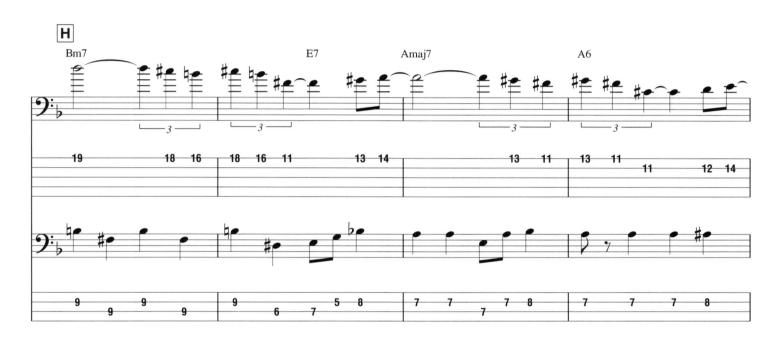

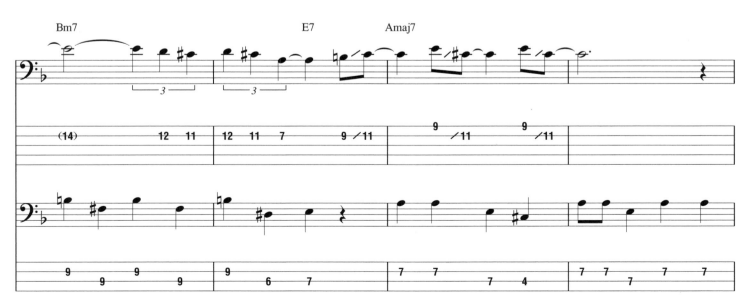

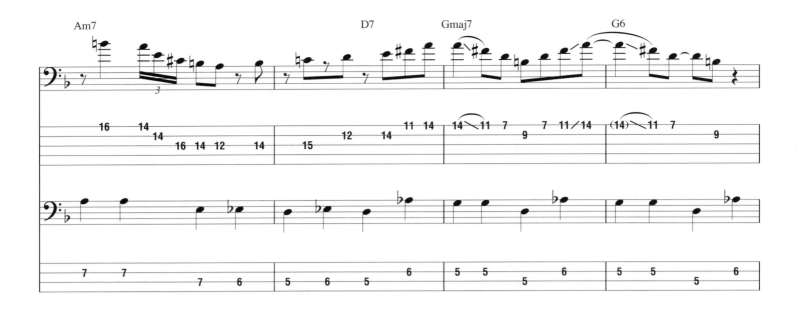

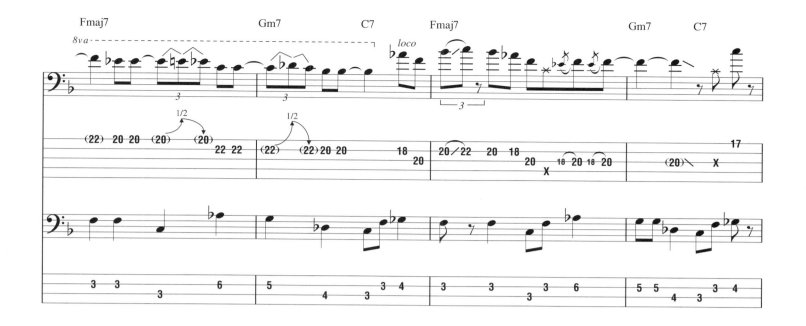

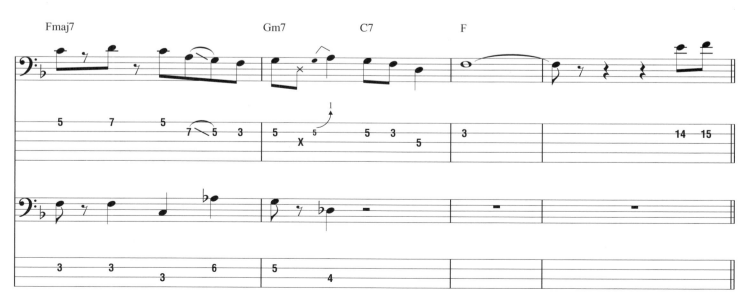

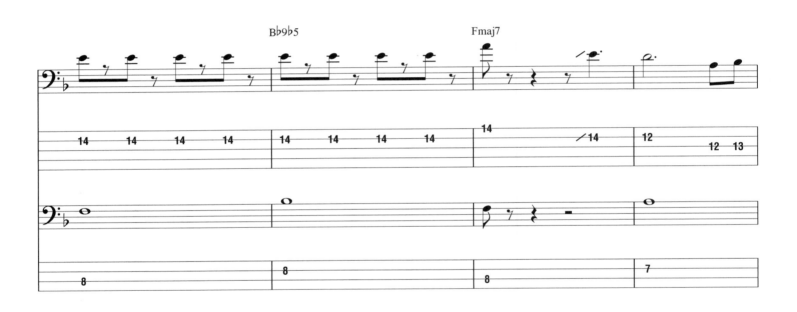

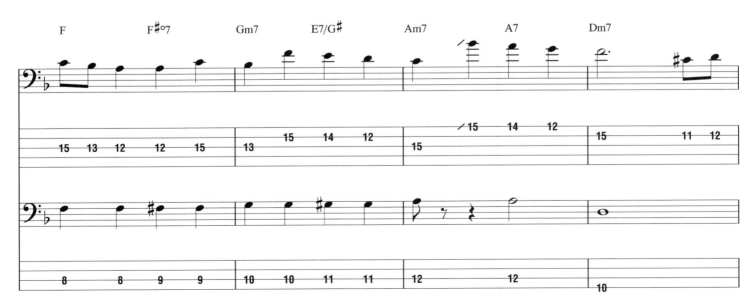

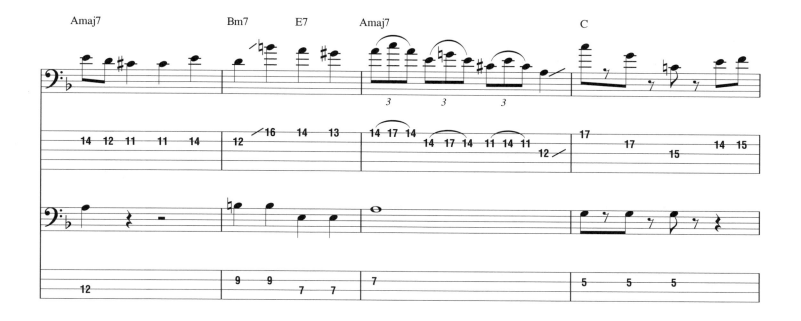

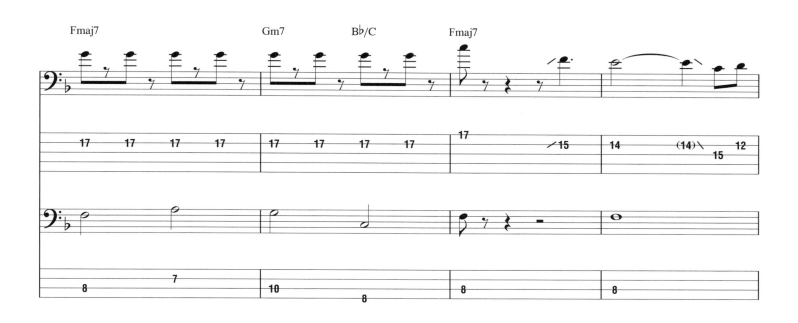

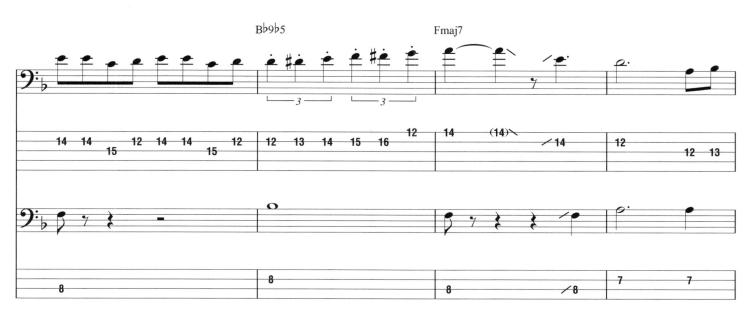

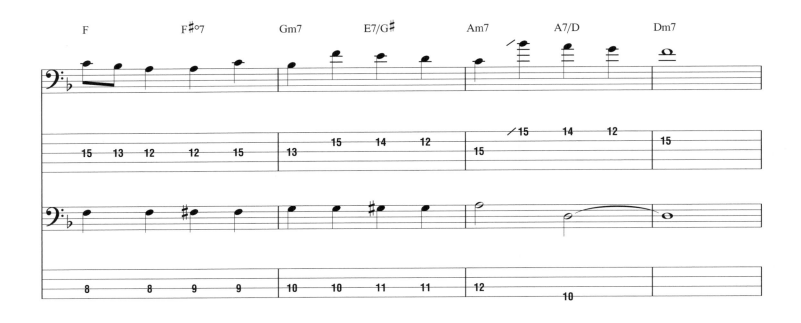

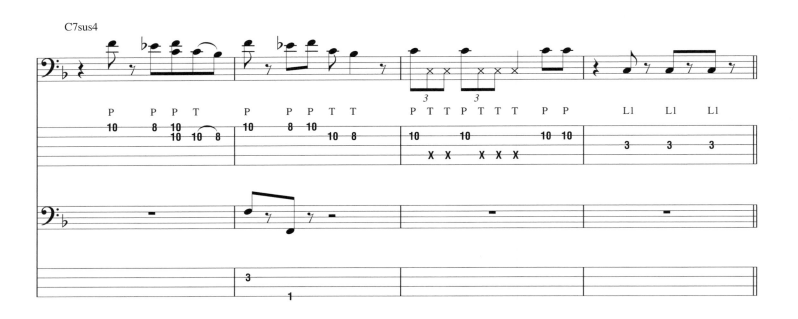

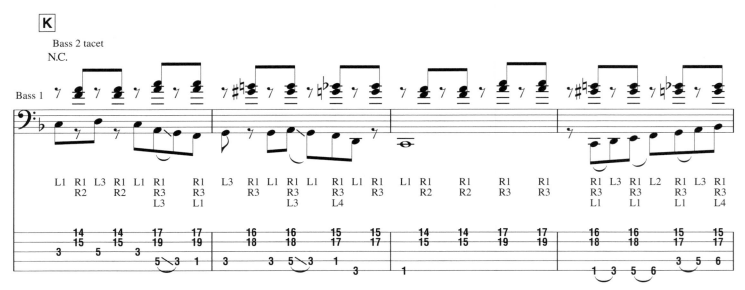

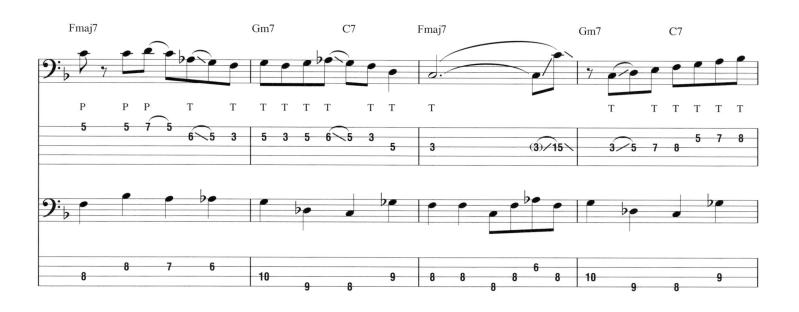

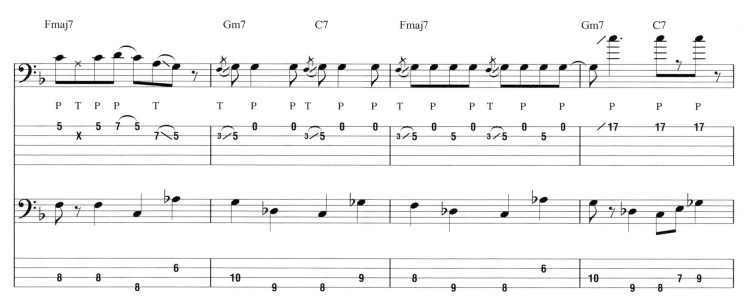

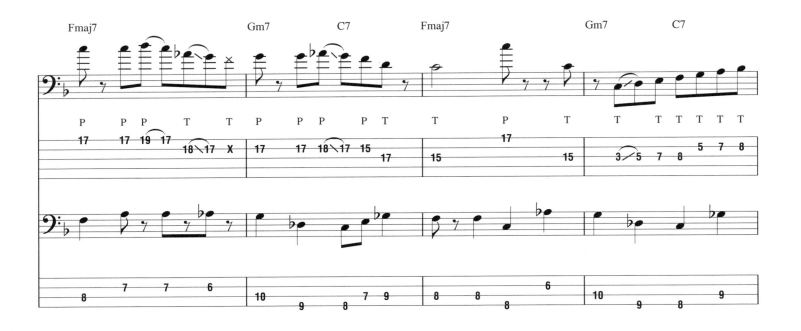

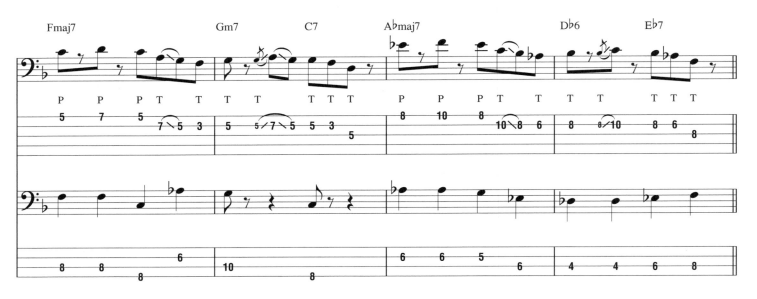

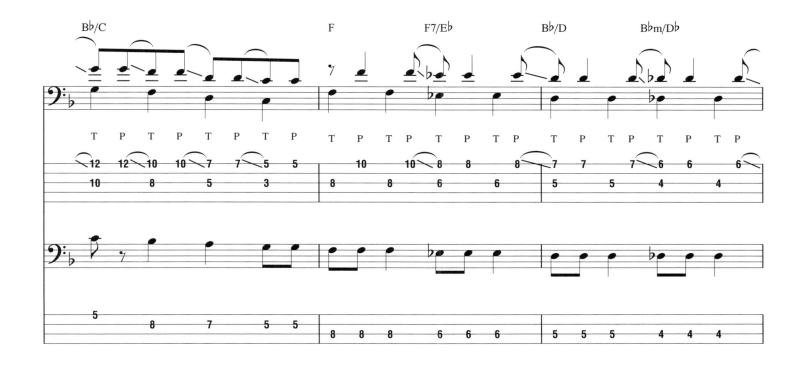

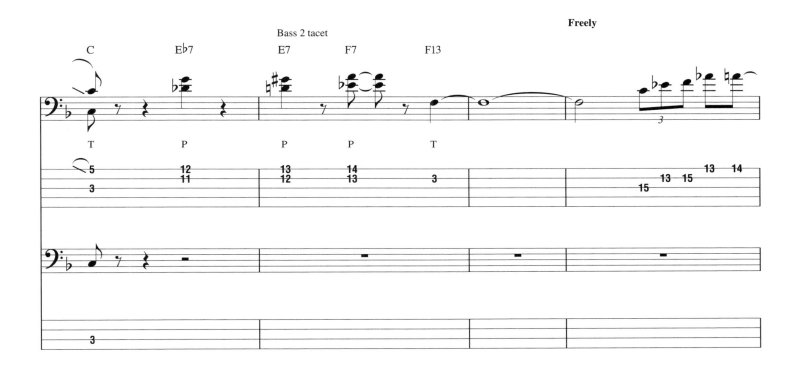

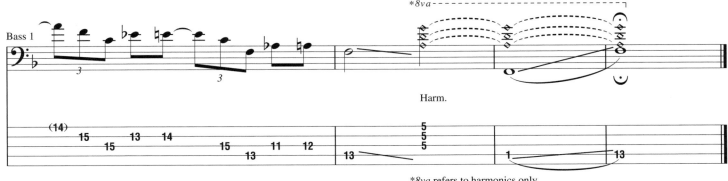

*8va refers to harmonics only.

TERMINAL BEACH

By Stuart Hamm

TREE

Music by Randy Coven

WHAT IS HIP

Words and Music by
Stephen Kupka, Emilio Castillo
and David Garibaldi

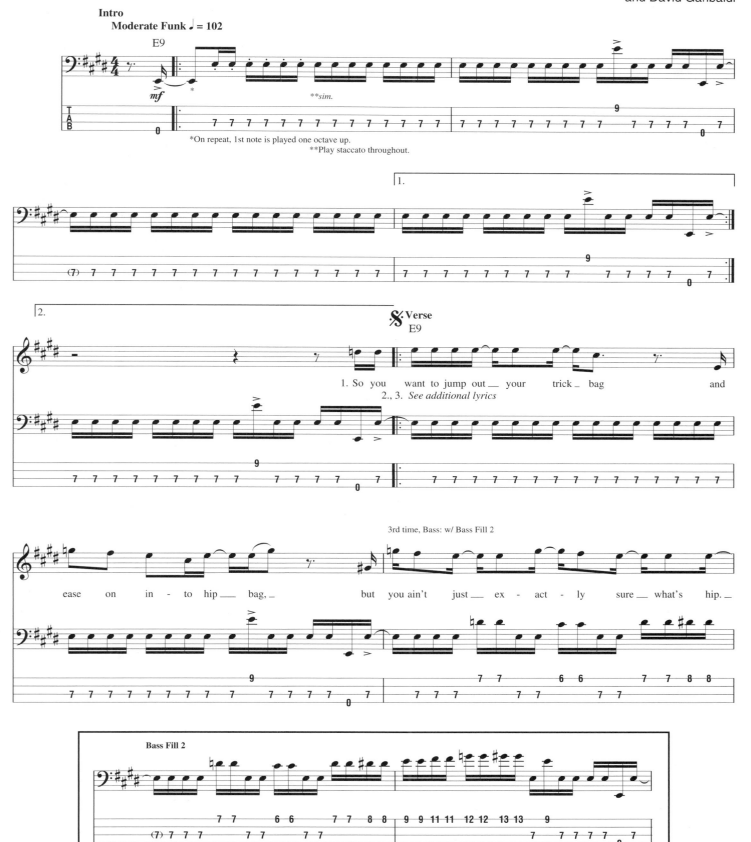

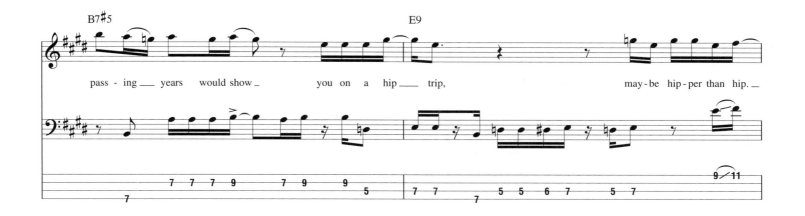

pass - ing ___ years would show ___ you on a hip ___ trip, may - be hip - per than hip. ___

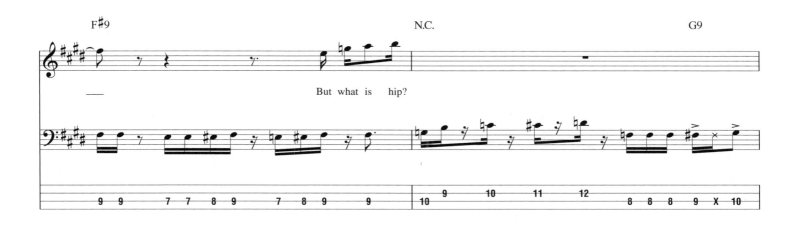

But what is hip?

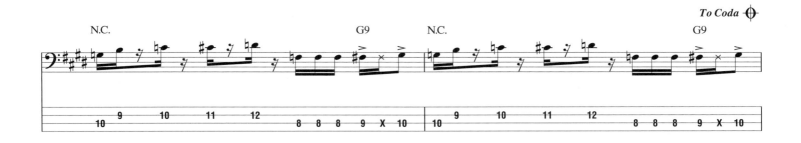

To Coda ⊕

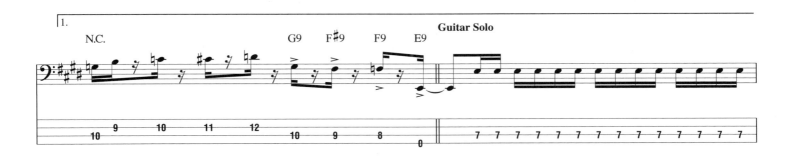

1.

Guitar Solo

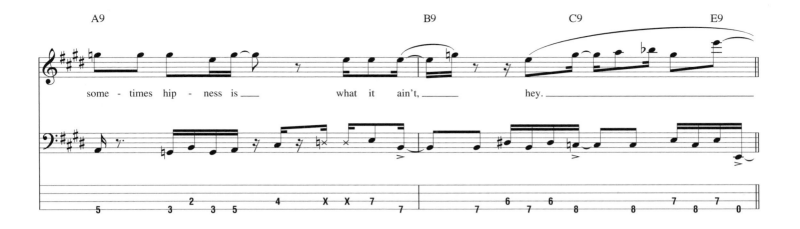

some - times hip - ness is ____ what it ain't, _____ hey. _____

Guitar Solo

D.S. al Coda

3. So you

⊕ Coda

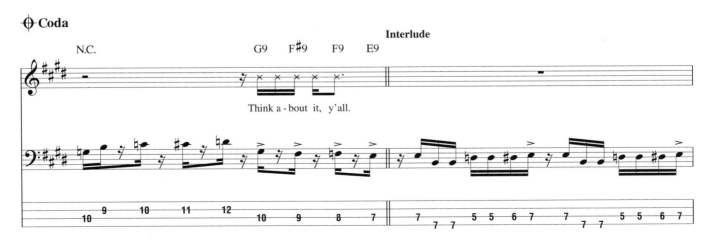

Think a - bout it, y'all.

pass - ing years_ will show,____ y'all.   What is   hip?____   Ah,_____

_____ y'all._____   What is   hip?____   I,_____   I'd   like   to   know._

____   What is   hip?____   Is   it   in ____   the   style _

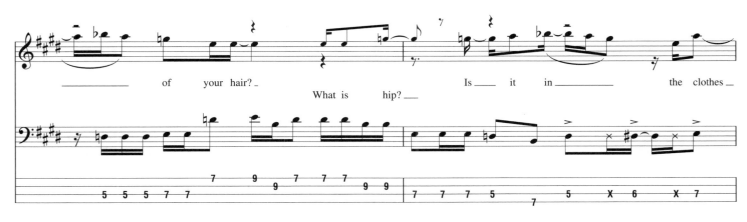

_____   of   your hair? _   What is   hip?____   Is ____ it   in _____   the   clothes _

that you ___ wear? _____ What is hip? ___ Ah, _____

_____ y'all. ___ Oh, I'd like __ to know __
What is hip? ___

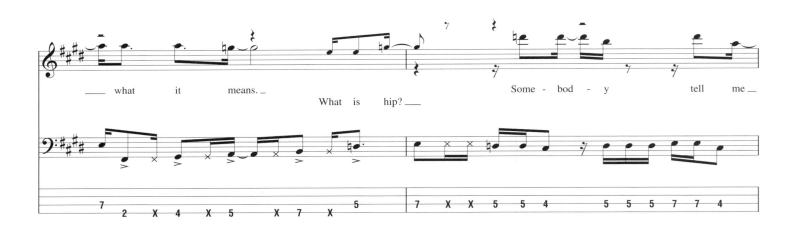

___ what it means. _ Some - bod - y tell me __
What is hip? ___

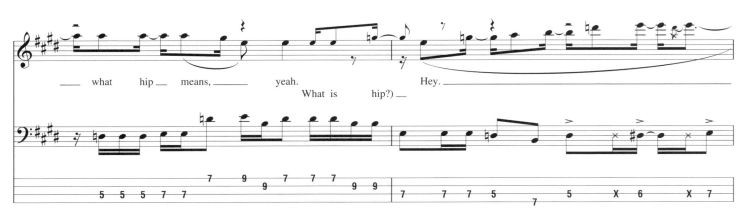

___ what hip __ means, _____ yeah. Hey. _____
What is hip?) ___

Additional Lyrics

2. So you became a part of the new breed, smokin' only the best weed,
   Hangin' out on the so-called hippest set.
   Seen at all the right places, seen with just the right faces.
   You should be satisfied but still it ain't quite right.*(To Chorus)*

3. So you went and found you a guru in an effort to find you a new you,
   And maybe even managed to raise your conscious level.
   Now you're starting to find the right road, there's one thing you should know.
   What's hip today might become passé.*(To Chorus)*

YOU CAN CALL ME AL

Words and Music by
Paul Simon

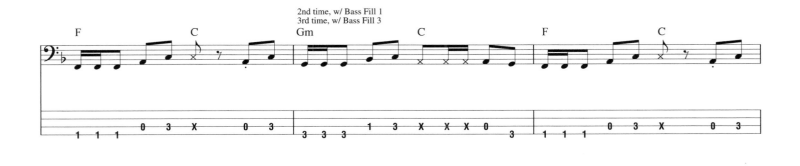

2nd time, w/ Bass Fill 1
3rd time, w/ Bass Fill 3

Chorus

*
If   you'll   be   my bod - y - guard...

*w/ fingers

Bass Fill 1

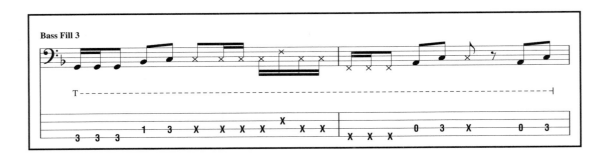

Bass Fill 3

To Coda ⊕

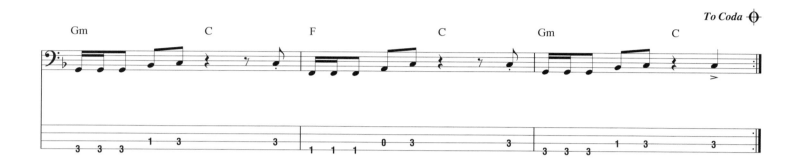

Penny Whistle Solo

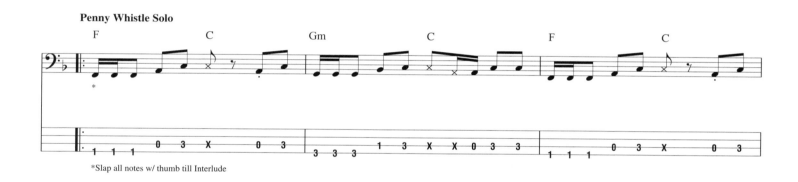

*Slap all notes w/ thumb till Interlude

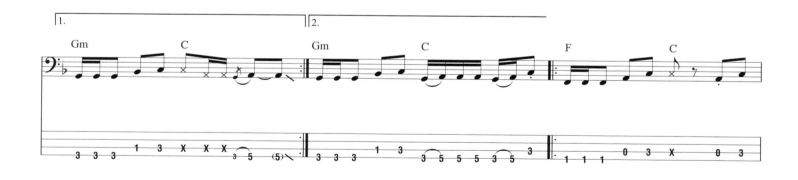

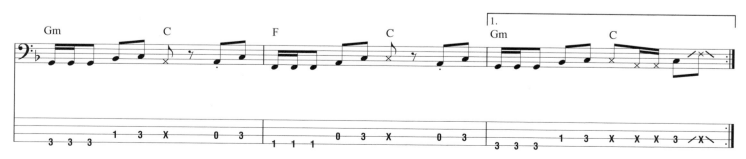

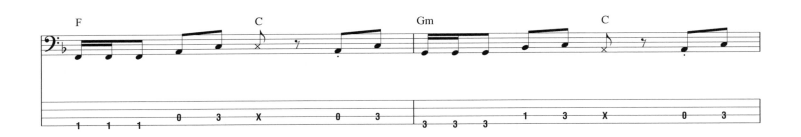

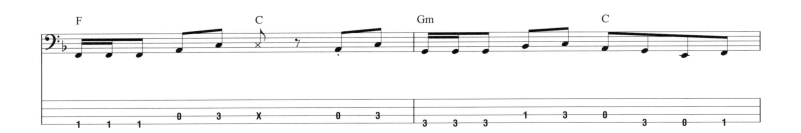

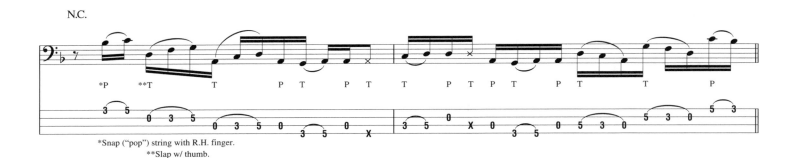

*Snap ("pop") string with R.H. finger.
**Slap w/ thumb.

Outro

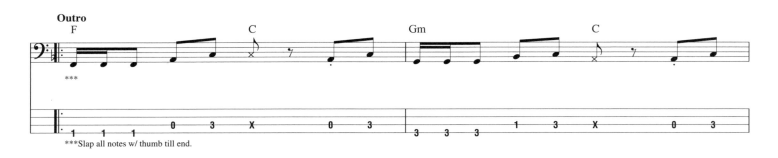

***Slap all notes w/ thumb till end.

Repeat and fade

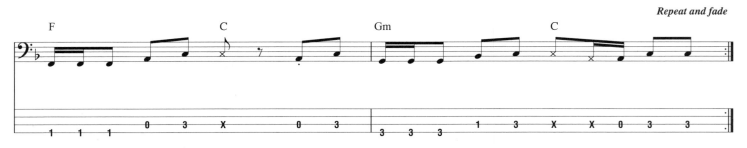